Managing Welfare Expectations and Social Change

Much has been written about the challenges Asian governments face in response to rapid socio-economic changes and the resulting social needs and welfare expectations. Indeed, heated debates have emerged when scholars in social development, social welfare and social policy conducted more systematic comparative research related to the diverse policy measures adopted by Asian governments: Which welfare models or typologies best describe Asian cases after the 2008 global financial crisis? How can contemporary social policy transformations in Asia be appropriately conceptualized? Are particular 'best practice' examples evolving in Asia and if so, can they be successfully transferred to enhance social welfare governance among Asian economies? This book combines contributions that address Asian government responses in light of the above questions. In doing so, it revisits the broad theoretical literature on 'policy transfer' and provides empirical examples to explore the spread of ideas, social policies and programmes across Asia from varying analytical and methodological perspectives.

The chapters originally published as a special issue in the *Journal of Asian Public Policy*.

Ka Ho Mok is Lam Man Tsan Chair Professor of Comparative Policy at Lingnan University, Hong Kong. He has extensive research experience in international higher education and comparative social policy with focus on Asia and contemporary China. He is Editor-in-Chief of *Journal of Asian Public Policy* (Routledge) and *Asian Education and Development Studies* (Emerald). He is also book series editor of Routledge series of *Comparative Development and Policy in Asia* and Palgrave Macmillan series of *Social Policy and Development Studies in East Asia*.

Stefan Kühner is Assistant Professor and Programme Director for the Master of Social Sciences in Comparative Social Policy (International), Department of Sociology and Social Policy, Lingnan University, Hong Kong. His academic interest centres on comparative and global social policy with particular emphasis on the policies and politics of productive and protective welfare.

Managing Welfare Expectations and Social Change

Policy Transfer in Asia

Edited by
Ka Ho Mok and Stefan Kühner

LONDON AND NEW YORK

First published 2018 by Routledge

2 Park Square, Milton Park, Abingdon, Oxfordshire OX14 4RN
52 Vanderbilt Avenue, New York, NY 10017

Routledge is an imprint of the Taylor & Francis Group, an informa business

First issued in paperback 2019

Copyright © 2018 Taylor & Francis

All rights reserved. No part of this book may be reprinted or reproduced or utilised in any form or by any electronic, mechanical, or other means, now known or hereafter invented, including photocopying and recording, or in any information storage or retrieval system, without permission in writing from the publishers.

Notice:
Product or corporate names may be trademarks or registered trademarks, and are used only for identification and explanation without intent to infringe.

British Library Cataloguing in Publication Data
A catalogue record for this book is available from the British Library

ISBN 13: 978-1-138-56404-6 (hbk)
ISBN 13: 978-0-367-89232-6 (pbk)

Typeset in MyriadPro
by diacriTech, Chennai

Publisher's Note
The publisher accepts responsibility for any inconsistencies that may have arisen during the conversion of this book from journal articles to book chapters, namely the possible inclusion of journal terminology.

Disclaimer
Every effort has been made to contact copyright holders for their permission to reprint material in this book. The publishers would be grateful to hear from any copyright holder who is not here acknowledged and will undertake to rectify any errors or omissions in future editions of this book.

Contents

Citation Information vii
Notes on Contributors ix

Introduction: Managing welfare expectations and social change: policy transfer in Asia 1
Ka Ho Mok and Stefan Kühner

1 Politics, power and policy transfer 8
Nick Ellison

2 Social policy diffusion in South Asia 25
Joachim Betz and Daniel Neff

3 India's emerging social policy paradigm: productive, protective or what? 40
Stefan Kühner and Keerty Nakray

4 Pension reform in Germany since the 1990s: new developments and theoretical implications 57
Liu Tao

5 Social decentralization: exploring the competitive solidarity of regional social protection in China 74
Shih-Jiunn Shi

6 East Asian welfare regime: obsolete ideal-type or diversified reality 90
Peter Abrahamson

7 East Asia in transition: re-examining the East Asian welfare model using fuzzy sets 104
Nan Yang

Index 121

Citation Information

The chapters in this book were originally published in the *Journal of Asian Public Policy*, volume 10, issue 1 (March 2017). When citing this material, please use the original page numbering for each article, as follows:

Introduction
Managing welfare expectations and social change: policy transfer in Asia
Ka Ho Mok and Stefan Kühner
Journal of Asian Public Policy, volume 10, issue 1 (March 2017) pp. 1–7

Chapter 1
Politics, power and policy transfer
Nick Ellison
Journal of Asian Public Policy, volume 10, issue 1 (March 2017) pp. 8–24

Chapter 2
Social policy diffusion in South Asia
Joachim Betz and Daniel Neff
Journal of Asian Public Policy, volume 10, issue 1 (March 2017) pp. 25–39

Chapter 3
India's emerging social policy paradigm: productive, protective or what?
Stefan Kühner and Keerty Nakray
Journal of Asian Public Policy, volume 10, issue 1 (March 2017) pp. 40–56

Chapter 4
Pension reform in Germany since the 1990s: new developments and theoretical implications
Liu Tao
Journal of Asian Public Policy, volume 10, issue 1 (March 2017) pp. 57–73

Chapter 5
Social decentralization: exploring the competitive solidarity of regional social protection in China
Shih-Jiunn Shi
Journal of Asian Public Policy, volume 10, issue 1 (March 2017) pp. 74–89

CITATION INFORMATION

Chapter 6
East Asian welfare regime: obsolete ideal-type or diversified reality
Peter Abrahamson
Journal of Asian Public Policy, volume 10, issue 1 (March 2017) pp. 90–103

Chapter 7
East Asia in transition: re-examining the East Asian welfare model using fuzzy sets
Nan Yang
Journal of Asian Public Policy, volume 10, issue 1 (March 2017) pp. 104–120

For any permission-related enquiries, please visit:
http://www.tandfonline.com/page/help/permissions

Notes on Contributors

Peter Abrahamson is Associate Professor of Sociology at University of Copenhagen, Denmark.

Joachim Betz is Professor Emeritus at the Institute of Political Science at the University of Hamburg, Germany.

Nick Ellison is Professor of Social Policy at the University of York, UK.

Stefan Kühner is Assistant Professor and Programme Director for the Master of Social Sciences in Comparative Social Policy (International), Department of Sociology and Social Policy, Lingnan University, Hong Kong.

Liu Tao is a Junior Professor at the Institute of East Asian Studies and at the Institute of Sociology in the Faculty of Social Sciences, University of Duisburg-Essen, Germany.

Ka Ho Mok is Lam Man Tsan Chair Professor of Comparative Policy at Lingnan University, Hong Kong.

Keerty Nakray is an Associate Professor at Jindal Global Law School in NCR Delhi, India and Visiting Fellow at the Feinstein International Center, Tufts University, USA.

Daniel Neff is Research Fellow at the GIGA Institute of Asian Studies, Germany.

Shih-Jiunn Shi is a Professor in the Graduate Institute of National Development, National Taiwan University, Taiwan.

Nan Yang is a PhD Graduand in the Department of Social Policy and Social Work at the University of York, UK.

INTRODUCTION

Managing welfare expectations and social change: policy transfer in Asia

Ka Ho Mok and Stefan Kühner

Introduction

Much has been written about the challenges Asian governments face in regards to growing welfare expectations and social change. High-income cases across Asia have been characterized as having to deal with external and internal pressures not unlike the ones experienced in OECD/EU countries (Taylor-Gooby 2009, Hemerjick 2013). At the economic level, globalization and technological change have increasingly led to the creation of 'new social risks' and – due to ensuing transitions in national production processes and labour markets – growing inequality and uncertainty (Hwang 2011, Izuhara 2013, Mok 2017). At the social level, changes in family structures and family life have – in conjunction with persistent gender inequality – contributed to low fertility rates and ageing populations putting significant pressures on social budgets particularly pensions, health and social care (Kim and Choi 2013, Sung and Pascall 2014; Ku 2016). New evidence suggests that governments in Greater China and East Asia face growing welfare expectations that go beyond the human capital-focused, family-oriented and work-centred approaches that have driven the welfare discourse after the 1997 and 2008 financial crises (Mok and Lau 2014, Ngok and Chan 2016). As for other Asian countries, debates have centred on concerns that recent socio-economic transitions threaten to 'trap' them in low- or middle-income status as large productivity gaps, imbalances in the key sources of economic growth, but also rising inequality, wage demands as well as environmental constraints continue to affect public and social policy making in the region (Surender and Walker 2013, Devine *et al.* 2015, Zhuang *et al.* 2015).

This Special Issue combines contributions that address Asian government responses in the light of the above transitions. It does so by revisiting the broad theoretical literature on 'policy transfer' and provides empirical examples to explore the spread of ideas, social policies and programmes across Asia from varying analytical and methodological perspectives. The impact of 'policy transfer' understood by Dolowitz and Marsh (1996, p. 344) as 'a process in which knowledge about policies, administrative arrangements, institutions etc. in one time and/or place is used in the development of policies, administrative arrangements and institutions in another time and/or place' has long been acknowledged in Western social policy analysis. In comparison, policy transfer explanations have played a much smaller role in Asian social policy analysis and have not commonly been referred to as an explanatory variable for Asian social policy development processes (Hudson *et al.* 2014). It is this knowledge gap that this Special Issue aims to begin to address.

Policy transfer: good practice but not copying

The earliest studies concerned with the way policies spread across time and space were largely committed to so-called prerequisites explanations, pointing to common conditions – usually the social or economic level of modernization – within states or nations, which arguably lead to the implementation of similar policies independently (Lipset 1959, Cutright 1963). Collier and Messick (1975) were among the first to go beyond this approach by arguing the implementation of social security policies in pioneer countries eventually led to conscious imitation by governments in other countries. Although these early quantitative approaches considerably added to the understanding of the many factors that precede, promote and accompany policy diffusion processes, its inability to answer central questions about the *subjective* side of action – that is, the motivations of policy makers to engage in policy imitation – and its systematic disregard of the specific historical and institutional environment in which *policy diffusion* takes place, eventually lead to a shift towards more case study approaches covering numerous policy areas (Hoberg 1991, Majone 1991; Wolman 1992, Dolowitz 1997).

Based on the lessons presented in these studies, Bennett (1991, p. 219) identified a 'tendency of societies to grow more alike, [and] to develop similarities in structures, processes and performances' by focusing on the general pattern of *policy convergence* between the policies adopted by national governments (for a more recent appraisal see: Heichel *et al.* 2005). Similarly, Rose (1991) focussed on the desirability and the practicability of *lesson drawing* from other countries, thus putting an emphasis on the voluntary decision of policy makers to adopt policies from abroad. The conceptual scope of *policy transfer* has been regarded as both broader and narrower than these related concepts. It is narrower in the sense that it is concerned with the transfer of specific ideas and policies and not with general relationships between internal and external factors and the transfer of policies. It is broader than these related concepts, as it is not only concerned with the transfer of policies as the result of decisions by actors inside the government, but also includes actors outside of it. For instance, Evans and Davies (1999, see also Evans 1999) underlined the link between emerging 'new governance' models (Rhodes 1996) and processes of *policy transfer* including the transfer of policies within nation states, for instance from one province to another. Stone (1999) pointed to the ability of regional and international organizations and transnational companies to push governments to adopt certain policies.

Meanwhile, representatives of the world polity school like Thomas Boli and John Meyer have made attempts to explore an independent level of global reality, which operates beyond national state borders (Boli and Thomas 1997; Meyer *et al.* 1997). As Liu and Sun (2016, p. 32) pointed out, '[they] have detected the emergence of a cosmopolitan world society, illuminating simultaneously a worldwide diffusion of rationalized models in the realm of high-school education, female education, environmental protection, competitive democracy, the institutions of the market economy, and so on'. Central to this school of thought is that the dissemination of values and rationalized models would induce a logical consequence of isomorphism. More specifically, triggered by the dominance of global ideas shaped at the international, not the national level, it is argued that 'the same institutional and structural development has taken place in almost all countries independent of the heterogeneous local cultural configuration and discrepancies in economic status at national and subnational levels' (Liu and Sun 2016, p. 32–33). Such a perspective provides an account for how ideas 'travel' around the world, particularly when national governments are under increasing pressure to identify 'good practices' elsewhere to inform policy making and enhance good governance.

Yet, it has also widely been argued that *policy transfer* must not be understood as an all-or-nothing process. Indeed, it is common place to suggest that governments have to adapt to political, cultural and socio-economic restrictions particularly if cross-national or even cross-regional policy transfer is the aim – in the majority of cases policy transfer must not be understood as simple 'copying' (Rose 1991). Even if a policy has met its expectations within one country and resulted in electoral success, this does not guarantee that it can be transferred effectively to another time or place. Similarly, a policy that looks like it meets all necessary requirements for successful policy transfer *on paper* may not be a practical solution to a given policy problem. In his analysis of the development of social security programmes under successive 'New Right' Conservative governments in Great Britain, the United States, Germany and Sweden during the 1980s and 1990s, Pierson (1994) famously demonstrated how existing institutional settings in each country determined the success or the failure of unpopular reforms. Maybe even more telling, Majone (1991) has forcefully illustrated how even as an occupying power, the United States failed to implement strict antitrust laws in Germany after WWII due to the opposition of the German industrial sector against such plans. Policy makers that engage in policy transfer must take seriously the question of fiscal affordability, but also whether technological prerequisites to implement a borrowed policy are within a country's capabilities and whether the bureaucrats that are meant to carry out the new legislation possess sufficient experience, motivation and the qualifications to do so (Lipsky 1979).

Several methodological challenges have been identified for research that engages in empirical explorations of policy transfer. First and foremost, as alluded to by Liu and Sun (2016), even if policies in different nations look alike, this does not necessarily mean this was the result of direct a deliberate policy transfer. A common suggestion has been that policy transfer explanations must demonstrate that policy makers were aware of other policy models and interested in them before they decided to engage in policy transfer – that is, only then can it be alleged with some certainty that policy transfer *actually happened*. The main problem is that direct interviews with policy makers involved in policy transfer are often not possible and policy transfer research tends to rely on secondary sources including mass media broadcasting materials, issued reports by research institutes, official statements and interviews by policy makers or official results of conferences and field visits. The risk with this approach is that policy makers may only borrow the *rhetoric* from other countries for office or vote seeking purposes without actually aiming to implement policies similar to their original. This might be the case, for instance, when policymakers have an interest in pointing to external necessities to diffuse their own responsibility for any possible negative outcomes of legislative changes (Vis 2016). On the other hand, policy makers may refuse to admit that they have learned from other countries, because they might have an interest in having their own name attached to a successful policy. The increased ability of policy makers to source information about policy programmes from evaluation studies published through the Internet and other related means of global communication might suggest that policy makers have become more independent from personal interactions than might have been the case in the past. It can be extremely difficult to establish whether policy makers had knowledge of a specific programme in concrete cases. The fact that the vast majority of instances of policy transfer are not one-to-one copies of existing *blueprints* makes this attempt even more complicated.

About this special issue

In extending upon these brief introductory remarks, *Ellison* – in the first contribution to this Special Issue – argues that important questions about the key processes, key actors (local, national and supranational) as well as their mutual power relations still remain unresolved. Rather than treating 'policy transfer' as a dependent variable, *Ellison* suggests that a focus on 'policy transfer' is more promising if regarded as an 'independent variable[s] capable of illuminating different components of policy analysis'. While not delivering a direct test of his ideal-typical model of power paradigms and policy transfer, the papers in this Special Issue address his call for 'more thorough case study material' to consider the explanatory power of policy transfer and should be regarded as an attempt not only to bring more Asian cases into the policy transfer literature more generally, but also – vice versa – to explore the extent to which empirical detail from Asian cases can be employed to further develop its conceptual apparatus.

The first empirical paper by *Betz and Neff* focuses on the introduction of rights-based employment guarantee programmes in South Asia and examine whether these might be attributed to processes of regional policy transfer. Indeed, they argue that socio-economic 'prerequisites' cannot fully explain the adoption of specific programme designs despite shared problem pressures such as persistent food insecurity and the failure of existing programmes to adequately deal with it. *Betz and Neff* argue that both the timing and the design of employment guarantee programmes in India, Nepal, Pakistan and Bangladesh owe much to political exigencies and the available administrative capacities of the countries. They also find evidence for the influence of external development actors as they actively promoted the successful Indian example as an inspiration for similar policy implementation. *Kühner and Nakray* also consider the effect of changes in the global academic discourse on economic development and the role of social protection on the international stage, but find relatively little evidence that India moved beyond its residual welfare policy approach during the successive Centre/Left Congress/United Progressive Alliance governments in the 2000s. While a series of innovative social policy innovations describe a concerted effort to shift the Indian welfare regime towards a more 'protective' centre of gravity, *Kühner and Nakray* suggest that these changes cannot be regarded as 'fully transformative' as they were hardly universal, largely failed to include special targeted measures for the most socially included and thus to contribute to improvements in productive asset creation among the poorest. In the Indian case, more genuine lesson drawing was hampered by a limited fiscal space, the role of individual states and the persistent importance of political patronage.

Lui moves away from South Asia to consider the theoretical implications of recent pension reform developments in Germany for the case of China. Traditionally characterized as ideal-typical Bismarckian, German pensions have undergone considerable changes since the 1990s with implications on the PAYG social insurance model and its traditionally gendered policy outcomes. While arguing that recent pension reform debates have been pushed and pulled by ideological differences within China, *Lui* suggests that policy learning – as was the case with Chinese statutory accident insurance since 2004 – would not only be possible but also instrumental to enable the emerging Chinese welfare regime to take greater account of gender-related imbalances that have so far been exacerbated by existing policies. *Shi* focuses on social decentralization within China to explore the competitive nature of regional social policy making. Rather than encouraging constructive cross-provincial 'policy learning' or 'lesson drawing', *Shi* emphasizes that the specific Chinese style central–local relationship has put in place complex processes that tend to lead to social dumping and regional protectionism which ultimately threaten any future efforts to create upward policy convergence of public goods and service provision.

The last two papers take a more comparative perspective to explore the development of the East Asian welfare model in recent years. *Abrahamson* revisits important debates about East Asian productivism and post-productivism, but focuses specifically on the proliferation of care policies in the region. Building on his previous work, which drew direct lines between the Danish experience in family policies and the development of care provision in Korea and China (Abrahamson 2014, 2015), *Abrahamson* sketches the key policy innovations in regards to parental leave, child and elderly care in China, Japan, Korea, Taiwan, Hong Kong and Singapore. While underlining the persistent role of Confucian ideals of filial piety, his discussion also reflects the different policy trajectories in regards to the care arrangements of individual cases in his study – that is, with some cases developing clearer conservative, some (potentially) liberal and other developmental/post-developmental features throughout these processes. The fact that an assessment of the path-breaking nature (or not) of East Asian cases is to a large part determined by the adjustment of one's analytical lens is also confirmed in the final paper by *Yang*, who challenges the productive welfare thesis by exploring education, health care, family, old-age pension, housing and protective labour market policy in China, Hong Kong, Japan, South Korea, Singapore and Taiwan. Using fuzzy-set ideal type analysis, *Yang* points out – yet again – that it is problematic to suggest that one homogeneous welfare model exists in East Asia. Despite some persistent similarities in the cultural foundations and general generosity of social policies, *Yang* illustrates an increasingly divergent pattern of welfare development across Greater China and East Asia often combining 'productive' and 'protective' social policies in unique ways.

Conclusion

This Special Issue was conceived against the wider context of strong needs for identifying good practices for policy transfer in order to promote better social policy making and governance in Asia. The (new) diversity in (East) Asian responses to the most pressing economic and social pressures may lead to more fruitful opportunities to engage in policy transfer moving forward. Given the magnitude of the shared experiences in an increasingly competitive and globalized world, it seems that – to quote *Ellison* one more time – 'developing a clear and systematic conceptual apparatus capable of explaining (at least) *how* policy is transferred, by *whom* (or through *what* structural mechanisms) and with *what effects*' (original *emphasis* by the original author) remains a fruitful endeavour for Asian social policy analysis. This Special Issue hopes to make a positive case and small contribution into this direction.

Most important of all, however, the empirical applications included in this Special Issue equally instruct us to be careful when analysing policy transfer projects conducted by national governments, especially when these national governments are sufficiently strong to drive the policy-making agendas and policy implementation through transnational diffusion of ideas, strategic policy learning or good practice adoption with careful national interpretations and adaptations. China is a case in point: while transnational ideas of welfare universalism and citizenship have clearly travelled to this giant state, the Chinese government has skilfully maintained its welfare pragmatism through the productivist construction of selective welfare capitalism despite facing pressures for further welfare provision (Mok).

Disclosure statement

No potential conflict of interest was reported by the authors.

References

Abrahamson, P., 2014. *Comparing social service system in Scandinavia and Korea and the directions of future development in Korea*. Gyeonggi: Gyeonggi Welfare Foundation.
Abrahamson, P., 2015. Gender and welfare regimes revisited: connecting Chinese and Danish perspectives. *Kvinder, Køn & Forskning*, 2015 (1), 67–79.
Bennett, C.J., 1991. what is policy convergence and what causes it? *British Journal of Political Science*, 21 (2), 215–233. doi:10.1017/S0007123400006116
Boli, J. and Thomas, G.M., 1997. World culture in the world polity: a century of international non-governmental organization. *American Sociological Review*, 62 (2), 171–190. doi:10.2307/2657298
Collier, D. and Messick, R., 1975. Prerequisites versus diffusion: testing alternative explanations of social security adoption. *American Political Science Review*, 69 (4), 1299–1315. doi:10.2307/1955290
Cutright, P., 1963. National political development: measurement and analysis. *American Sociological Review*, 28 (2), 253–264. doi:10.2307/2090612
Devine, J., Kühner, S., and Nakray, K., 2015. Meeting emerging global policy challenges: positioning social policy between development and growth? *Journal of International and Comparative Social Policy*, 31 (2), 95–99. doi:10.1080/21699763.2015.1052835
Dolowitz, D. and Marsh, D., 1996. Who learns what from whom: a review of the policy transfer literature. *Political Studies*, 44 (2), 343–357. doi:10.1111/j.1467-9248.1996.tb00334.x
Dolowitz, D., 1997. British employment policy in the 1980s: learning from the American experience. *Governance*, 10 (1), 23–42. doi:10.1111/gove.1997.10.issue-1
Evans, M., 1999. Policy transfer networks and collaborative government: the case of social security fraud. *Public Policy and Administration*, 14 (2), 30–48. doi:10.1177/095207679901400204

Evans, M. and Davies, J., 1999. Understanding policy transfer: a multi-level, multi-disciplinary perspective. *Public Administration*, 77 (2), 361–385. doi:10.1111/padm.1999.77.issue-2

Heichel, S., Pape, J., and Sommerer, T., 2005. Is there convergence in convergence research? An overview of empirical studies on policy convergence. *Journal of European Public Policy*, 12 (5), 817–840. doi:10.1080/13501760500161431

Hemerjick, A., 2013. *Changing welfare states*. Oxford: Oxford University Press.

Hoberg, G., 1991. Sleeping with an elephant: the American influence on Canadian environmental regulation. *Journal of Public Policy*, 11 (1), 107–132. doi:10.1017/S0143814X00004955

Hudson, J., Kühner, S., and Yang, N., 2014. Productive welfare, the East Asian 'model' and beyond: placing welfare types in greater china into context. *Social Policy and Society*, 13 (2), 301–315. doi:10.1017/S1474746413000572

Hwang, G.J., ed., 2011. *New welfare states in East Asia: global challenges and restructuring*. London: Edward Elgar.

Izuhara, M., 2013. *Handbook on East Asian social policy*. Cheltenham: Edward Elgar.

Kim, J.W. and Choi, Y.J., 2013. Farewell to old legacies? The introduction of long-term care insurance in South Korea. *Ageing and Society*, 33, 871–887. doi:10.1017/S0144686X12000335

Ku, Y.W., 2016. East Asian Welfare regime revisited: what changes in the 21st century? In: *Paper presented at the Postgraduate Studies Seminar Series, Lingnan University*, 31 March 2016 Hong Kong.

Lipset, S.M., 1959. Some social requisites of democracy: economic development and political legitimacy. *American Political Science Review*, 53 (1), 69–105. doi:10.2307/1951731

Lipsky, M., 1979. *Street-level bureaucracy*. New York: Russel Sage Foundation.

Liu, T. and Sun, L., 2016. Urban social assistance in China: transnational diffusion and national interpretation. *Journal of Current Chinese Affairs*, 2, 25–51.

Majone, G., 1991. Cross-national sources of regulatory policy making in Europe and the United States. *Journal of Public Policy*, 11 (1), 79–106. doi:10.1017/S0143814X00004943

Meyer, J., et al., 1997. World society and the nation-state. *American Journal of Sociology*, 51 (4), 623–651.

Mok, K.H. and Lau, M., eds., 2014. *Managing social change and social policy in Greater China. Welfare regimes in transition*. London: Routledge.

Mok, K.H., ed., 2017. *Managing international connectivity, diversity of learning and changing labour markets: east Asian perspectives*. Singapore: Springer.

Ngok, K.L. and Chan, C.K., eds., 2016. *China's social policy: transformation and challenges*. Abingdon: Routledge.

Pierson, P., 1994. *Dismantling the welfare state? Reagan, thatcher and the politics of retrenchment*. Cambridge: Cambridge University Press.

Rhodes, R.A.W., 1996. The new governance: governing without government. *Political Studies*, 44, 652–667. doi:10.1111/j.1467-9248.1996.tb01747.x

Rose, R., 1991. What is lesson-drawing? *Journal of Public Policy*, 11 (1), 3–30. doi:10.1017/S0143814X00004918

Stone, D., 1999. Learning lessons and transferring policy across time, space and disciplines. *Politics*, 19 (1), 51–59. doi:10.1111/1467-9256.00086

Sung, S. and Pascall, P., eds., 2014. *Gender and welfare states in East Asia: confucianism or gender equality*. London: Palgrave/MacMillan.

Surender, R. and Walker, R., eds., 2013. *Social policy in a developing world*. Cheltenham: Edward Elgar.

Taylor-Gooby, P., 2009. *Reframing social citizenship*. Oxford: Oxford University Press.

Zhuang, J., Vandenberg, P., and Huang, Y., 2015. *Managing the middle-income transition. Challenges facing the People's Republic of China*. Cheltenham: Edward Elgar.

Vis, B., 2016. Taking stock of the comparative literature on the role of blame avoidance strategies in social policy reform. *Journal of Comparative Policy Analysis: Research and Practice*, 18 (2), 122–137. doi:10.1080/13876988.2015.1005955

Wolman, H., 1992. Understanding cross-national policy transfers: the case of Britain and the US. *Governance*, 5 (1), 27–45. doi:10.1111/gove.1992.5.issue-1

RESEARCH ARTICLE

Politics, power and policy transfer

Nick Ellison

ABSTRACT
Although the extensive literature on policy transfer and learning has succeeded in raising awareness of the myriad issues associated with this complex field, the goal of developing a clear and systematic conceptual apparatus capable of explaining (at least) *how* policy is transferred, *by whom* (or *through what* structural mechanisms) and with *what effects* has so far proved elusive. This verdict is not in fact surprising because, as the literature demonstrates, 'policy transfer' is characterized by contested definitional and conceptual debates, inherently complex contextual detail, and challenging methodological problems, which together conspire to limit the scope and impact of theoretical insights and empirical findings. Nevertheless, despite these difficulties, it is possible to utilize what is a sophisticated and insightful literature in a different manner. Rather than treat policy transfer as a dependent variable, it is advantageous to understand the term as an integral component of the wider field of policy analysis and one that can throw light on a range of policy issues. The role of power in policymaking – and specifically the differential operation of power relations in a globalizing world – is one area that an appreciation of the complex dynamics of policy transfer can illuminate. Following a review of the core debates concerning policy transfer, this article goes on to argue that different power paradigms can be associated with different types of transfer process. An appreciation of the characteristics of these paradigms makes it possible to develop a model that depicts the interaction of power and policy transfer at different levels and spatial scales.

1. Introduction

Despite the plethora of articles about 'policy transfer'[1] in recent years, there is a danger that debates in this area of policy studies have generated more heat than light. Although the literature contains significant insights into the processes and mechanisms by and through which something called 'policy' is somehow 'learned', 'transferred', 'diffused' or 'emulated', the overriding impression is of an area that is so complex, and in which variables are both so mutable and extensive, that it becomes virtually impossible to produce an acceptable level of explanatory parsimony. As Dunlop and Radaelli (2013, p. 600) have commented recently, '... even the most casual of observers would note that the field is struggling to produce systematic and cumulative knowledge on this topic'. In view of these conceptual and empirical difficulties, it is important to ask two fundamental questions. First, *why* is this field so apparently complex and, second, how might it be possible to use the literature to illuminate key issues about policy-making that incorporate, but go beyond, the relatively narrow concerns of policy transfer? The particular issue of interest for this article concerns the differential uses of power in policy processes in which forms of transfer and learning play a significant role. Power relations are, of course, discussed implicitly and, on occasion, explicitly (Dolowitz and Marsh 1996, 2000, Evans 2009, Hudson and Lowe 2009) throughout the literature, although transfer as 'coercion' has perhaps not been given as much detailed conceptual space as other more consensual versions of transfer. This deficit is particularly stark in areas of global social policy where power inequalities between major global institutions, often supported by core metropolitan economies, on the one hand, and developing economies, on the other, lead to programmes being effectively imposed or potential benefits being made conditional on specific performance. Before turning to this issue, however, it is important to clarify and explore some of the claims being made here. What have been the main contributions to the field of policy transfer to date? What are the strengths and drawbacks of these approaches?

2. Policy transfer: key issues

It is possible to understand the policy learning literature over the past 20 years or so as engaged in a debate that, at its core, contains two different sets of assumptions – one that understands policy transfer as an essentially rational process that is itself open to rational enquiry and one that believes it to be inherently messy, incremental and potentially 'irrational'. The more rational policy transfer is held to be, the greater the temptation to treat it as a dependent variable. Rose (1991, p. 22), for example, sees rationality in policy transfer, or 'lesson-drawing' as he calls it, as a potential range of processes through which policies can either be copied, emulated, hybridized, synthesized or inspired (Rose 1991, p. 22) in ways that permit 'steps [to] be taken to make a programme effective in one country today succeed elsewhere tomorrow' (Rose 1991, p. 24). Researching these processes in Rose's view, could make it possible to predict whether 'a programme now in effect in country X would be effective if transferred to country Y' (Rose 1991, p. 8). Underpinning this approach is the assumption that whether policies are directly copied, 'emulated' or merely inspired by developments elsewhere, the *processes* involve a logical sequence with actors starting with problem identification, scanning programmes elsewhere, adapting programmes to local requirements and conducting a prospective evaluation of likely success. The implication is that these processes are open to 'measurement' and modelling with the hope that – at the least – a comprehensive model of policy transfer can be developed.

A different and wider-ranging approach that nevertheless assumes that policy transfer has a rational character can be seen in the seminal contributions of Dolowitz and Marsh (1996, 2000). For these contributors, the main aim was to provide a clear framework within which the various processes associated with policy transfer could be itemized and analysed. The key questions posed by Dolowitz and Marsh belie an assumption that the transfer process is rational because the process is imagined as a logical series of steps with a beginning and an end, a finite range of actors involved and contextualized by a number of exogenous factors, including those that determine whether a particular transfer process is voluntary or coercive. Of particular significance for Dolowitz and Marsh (2000, p. 8) were questions about why actors engaged in policy transfer, who these actors might be, what was being transferred, from where, the degrees of transfer were involved, and whether the transfer process itself could be considered a success or failure.

There is no doubting the influence of these contributions. By framing the questions about policy transfer in this way, Dolowitz and Marsh provided a research agenda that is of continuing relevance (see Benson and Jordan 2011). That said, the approach has not been deemed entirely satisfactory. As pointed out in note 1, 'policy transfer' was used by Dolowitz and Marsh (1996, 2000) as a generic term that contained concepts ranging from the voluntarism associated with Rose's lesson-drawing, through structural accounts of policy diffusion (e.g. Simmons and Elkins 2004) to others that combine structure and agency to produce sophisticated analyses of particular transfer events (see Fawcett and Marsh 2012). For Evans and Davies (1999, p. 365), 'the framework developed by Dolowitz and Marsh is clearly designed to incorporate a vast domain of policy-making activity by classifying all possible occurrences of transfer, voluntary and coercive, temporal and spatial'. However, this all-encompassing approach means that no robust *theory* of policy transfer is advanced. As Evans and Davies (1999, p. 364 original emphasis) argue, the framework is unable 'to determine with *precision* the phenomenon it is trying to explain'. To move on from this point, Evans and Davies developed a multilevel, multidisciplinary perspective that takes greater account of the prevailing conditions or contexts within which policy transfer takes place, including a greater appreciation of the structure–agency relationship and, in particular, the ways in which policy transfer networks as temporary transfer agents both condition, and are conditioned by, structural forces associated with global, transnational and international movements and institutions.

Although Evans and Davies attempted to provide a clearer account of the key factors involved in policy transfer, one result of their analytical approach has been to point up just how complex transfer processes actually are. It is interesting that in his more recent writing, Evans (2010, p. 159) continues to reflect on the theoretical and methodological difficulties involved in developing a robust model, noting that 'much of the existing literature does not provide adequate techniques for demonstrating policy transfer'. In many ways, this verdict is not surprising. If the transfer literature has a particular strength, it lies in its ability to identify the complexities of a highly pluralized field. If it has a weakness, it is an inability to push beyond this exploration of parameters and content to accounts of transfer that are theoretically coherent, methodologically sound and consequently able to inform the conduct of transfer events. This weakness is significant because the absence of a compelling model of transfer raises the possibility that such a model is chimerical. It may be less a question of discovering adequate techniques to measure policy transfer somehow, as Evans would have it, and more one of accepting that the continuing investigation of this area of policy studies is likely to produce more questions than answers. Going further, it is important to retain something of Lindblom's (1959, 1979) understanding of policymaking as an incremental process of 'muddling through'; going further still, it is not fanciful to perceive policy transfer and learning as a field in which the key players 'nick stuff from all over the place' (Dwyer and

Ellison 2009, see also Stone 2012) using only the outermost bounds of bounded rationality as metaphorical route markers.

Although this conclusion may not appear to be particularly rewarding, at least for those who continue to hope for an all-encompassing theory, much can be derived from successive analyses of policy transfer that build knowledge incrementally – and indeed adapt to the ever-changing conditions of policy development – over time. By ceasing to treat policy transfer as a dependent variable, it becomes possible to use the insights produced by policy transfer analysis to explore key dimensions of the ever-changing and increasingly global policy process – one such dimension being power, as discussed below.

What, then, are the key problems that make policy transfer as a dependent variable so difficult to 'measure'? This is not in itself a new question and efforts to answer it have consistently been attempted by Evans (2009), Marsh and Evans (2012), Stone (1999, 2004, 2012) and many others. A swift recap of the core issues is important, however, partly because it provides a snapshot of the current state of knowledge and partly because it exposes key lacunae in the literature that signal a need to reassess contemporary understandings of the field. Arguably, the main inhibitions to the production of a comprehensive account of policy transfer concern the innate complexity, and in some respects the essential contestability, of three key dimensions: the structural and/or institutional origins of any transfer; what it is that is being transferred; and the range of actors involved, including institutional actors. There are, of course, other questions that could be included in this kind of policy analysis, the issue of policy convergence being one (Holzinger and Knill 2005, Knill 2005), but this matter stands somewhat to one side of the issues being pursued here.

3. Origins, policies and actors

It is helpful to categorize transfer processes as either 'exogenous' or 'endogenous', although these categories are not always entirely discrete. Exogenously derived transfers may be coercive or consensual in nature and have a common feature in their point of origin being combinations of structural forces, and sets of actors, which stand outside the immediate transfer locus. Pressures – often global and economic – can occur outside a particular arena and trigger subsequent learning and transfer activities within this particular universe of institutions and actors. There may also be feedback effects by which policies that owe much to the impact of exogenous institutions, actors and ideas, may be altered in the course of domestic shaping and implementation in ways that have a recursive impact on these original sources of change. 'Coercive' transfers, for example, frequently originate in ideas and policy prescriptions developed by key global institutions, but these institutions themselves vary in character and the policies they prescribe change over time (Mahon 2010). Global institutions like the International Monetary Fund (IMF) or the World Bank (WB) operate alongside other influential transnational actors including powerful nation states, epistemic communities and private sector interests. Of course, transnational transfers need not be purely coercive. Consensual transfers occur, for example, where national governments accept aid or other support programmes conditional upon meeting mutually agreed targets negotiated with global institutions (Orenstein 2009) – although, as discussed below, the detail lies in the nature of power relations and the relative strengths and weaknesses of parties to the bargaining process. Rather differently, what may be thought of as global 'discussion-chains' – international conferences, policy summits and so on – can also lead to policy programmes that become objects of negotiation with national governments.

Exogenous pressures for policy transfer can also originate within regional organizations such as the European Union, MERCOSUR, ASEAN or the African Union operating in an institutional frame that includes national governments and other national actors, the regional agencies of global institutions, and regional policy networks. Depending on the nature of the institutions involved – and regional bodies vary considerably in power and influence – they can either coercively drive or facilitate policy transfer in areas such as labour market policy, health policy, security policy and aspects of social policy. Regional institutions can also transfer policies and 'learn' among themselves (Farrell 2009).

Endogenous forms of transfer may appear a contradiction in terms. After all, the idea of 'transfer' implies that something is imported from 'outside' into a different arena. While it is true that the identification of the need for change is likely to stem from an awareness of shifts and movements caused by a range of external forces and actors, it is nevertheless the case that the impetus behind decisions to implement new policies or embrace new ideas can originate endogenously in perceptions of policy failure, or pressures created, for example, by domestic institutional change. Endogenous transfer processes are more obviously associated with policy transfers between nation states where national governments have themselves identified a need for new policies or the improvement of existing ones in response to emerging political demands or perceived policy failures. Typically, the countries involved come from the wealthier parts of the world and tend to enjoy relatively close social, political and cultural ties. There are numerous studies of policy transfer among core Organization for Economic Cooperation and Development (OECD) countries such as the U.S.A., the U.K., Germany, Australia and Sweden in which the clear desire to 'learn from abroad' is accompanied by the internal recognition of policy deficits (e.g. Dwyer and Ellison 2009; Deacon 2000; Daguerre and Taylor-Gooby 2004; Daguerre 2007; Cebulla 2005; Fawcett and Marsh 2012).

Turning to 'what' is transferred, it is important, following Stone (2004), to distinguish between 'soft' and 'hard' forms of transfer. In a context where global institutions are involved and where power relations are unequal, (exogenous) pressures from these institutions targeted at national governments in developing economies can take the form of the hard transfer or imposition of economic strategies and the policies associated with them. Arguably there is less room for contingency here – certainly those contingencies associated with interventions from non-state actors such as informal policy networks and private interests that feature in soft transfer processes. While it is certainly possible for policies, and indeed institutions, to be transferred wholesale from country A to country B – and some of the studies mentioned above specifically explored examples relating to the spread of Active Labour Market Policies in the wealthier OECD countries – the exact replication of a policy in a different country is hard to achieve. Difficulties preventing any simple transfer of this kind include the degree of resistance to change, or problems associated with 'translation'.

Where resistance is encountered – or simply where the play of historical, bureaucratic or cultural assumptions and practices militates against simple adoption – 'what' is transferred may be something less than a fully defined policy. It may be, for instance, that particular types of legislation or regulatory tools are transferred. Stone (2012, p. 486) refers to 'the spread and adoption of Freedom of Information Law and the Ombudsman's office' in this respect. Again, ideas and knowledge that 'inform' policy discussions while not prescribing specific policy outcomes can be imported in a number of ways – for example, through formal interactions among government officials or through the spread of new ways of thinking through informal policy networks. If ideas and discourse are important factors in policy transfer (Schmidt and Radaelli 2004, Béland 2005) practices, or 'ways of doing things', may also be learned and lead over time to policy developments that mimic or emulate the spirit of practices elsewhere without their accompanying institutional frameworks. Massey's (2009, p. 388) observation that 'all policy transfer is in reality policy mimesis' acknowledges that the boundaries of the 'what' of policy transfer can be porous, the further implication being that transfer routes and pathways can be hard to trace. Of course, the 'softer' the type of transfer and the more voluntary and consensual the processes are, the more difficult it becomes to measure precisely what has been transferred, let alone the impact or success of the transfer itself.

'Actors' involved in policy transfer can be institutions, policy networks or influential individuals. If at one time, there was an assumption that national or subnational governmental institutions and networks, peopled by national politicians, leading civil servants and key policy entrepreneurs were the main players in transfer processes, the recognition that 'globalization' has increased the spatial scale of play has led to a growing awareness of the vast range of interests and agencies involved, including new actors and new modes of governance (Crozier 2008; O'Brien 2009). As mentioned, leading global and regional institutions have come to be regarded as significant transfer agents – to the point where some observers now argue that these institutions are fundamentally reshaping the policies and policy processes of 'sovereign' nation states (Hameiri and Jones 2016). Elsewhere, attention has been drawn to the role of global policy networks and epistemic communities, transnational corporations and other privately funded networks and foundations that, with the increase in global communications and removal of controls on capital movement are able to exert either 'hard' or 'soft' power and influence (Stone 2004, 2010) on policymakers.

This brief summation of the main questions and debates in the policy transfer literature indicates the problems of depicting policy transfer as a bounded entity that allows it to be treated as a dependent variable. From difficult definitional issues, through problems associated with the scope and reach, and the what and who of transfer, the variables involved are extensive and the measurement of their influence too methodologically challenging to allow the development of a comprehensive, empirically testable explanatory model. However, what may be considered a weakness of the field in some respects arguably becomes a strength in others. By treating policy transfer as an independent variable capable of manifestation in varying sets of processes, the literature can be used to explore the role of other relevant factors in the transfer process and particularly the ways in which these intrinsic components of transfer can 'mutually condition' one another. The utilization and deployment of 'power' is a leading issue here because, with the dramatic expansion of transfer (voluntary and coercive) on a global scale, the recognition of the central importance of this concept facilitates a clearer, multilevel understanding of 'transfer politics'. Of course, power permeates all aspects of policymaking but the point here is that a focus on policy transfer will illuminate particular dimensions of power and influence, particularly at global level. The following section examines how policy transfer analysis can expose the role and nature of power – and how, conversely, an understanding of power can enhance understandings of key aspects of transfer.

4. Policy transfer and power

Power is an essentially contested concept in the social sciences as Lukes' classic discussion of the idea convincingly demonstrates (Gallie 1956, Lukes 1974). Although its contestability means that the concept has to be treated carefully, in terms of policy transfer the key issues concern degrees of 'coercion', 'conditionality' and 'influence', these categories intersecting with varieties of 'hard' and 'soft' power discussed by Stone and others. It is obviously important to treat the concept of power in a nuanced manner. The policy transfer literature takes account of very different sources and concentrations of power, from transnational and national institutions through to formal and informal policy networks, and corporate interests (see Adam and Kriesi 2007). In so doing, it provides a space to examine the complex interactions among different forms of power and different types of transfer. Certainly for present purposes, power should not be treated as a zero-sum phenomenon but rather as a fluid quantity capable of shifting in concentration depending on a range of factors including prevailing social and political contexts and the global economic environment. On this reading, the policy transfer literature can be said to utilize three ideal typical paradigmatic forms of power in its analyses of transfer processes: 'power as mutual influence' (PMI) through voluntary or open learning; 'power as weighted bargaining' (PWB) and 'power as coercion and/or conditionality'. The important thing is that these paradigms contribute to an understanding of how different forms of power can be associated with different transfer processes in different environments.

4.1 *Power as mutual influence (PMI)*

Power is best conceived in terms of 'influence' in this paradigm. The main characteristic of the paradigm is mutuality and the consensual (and largely endogenous) recognition that existing policies and programmes can be improved by attending to developments elsewhere. It is important, however, to treat 'influence' as a form of power because many of the debates about policy transfer within and among institutions, actors and networks, particularly among the wealthier Western nations, are largely concerned with discussions among 'equals' with participants not disadvantaged by significant power asymmetries. It is not surprising that OECD countries that are economically, socially, politically and culturally 'close' engage in forms of transfer that are largely voluntary and open, and where 'influence' is less an exercise of power *per se* and more about persuasion and debate in a context of open learning and adaptation. Of course, overall context is important and even where the initial stimulus for policy transfer is endogenous, policy preferences are subject to 'fashion' and shifts in macropolitical agendas (True *et al.* 2007). Nevertheless, in a pluralist environment in which influence is relatively diffused within and across key institutions and actors, the precise configuration of actors, degrees of institutionalization and relative influence of formal and informal policy networks and communities will bear heavily on outcomes. This statement needs to be interrogated a little further, however, because much depends on matters of scope and reach. Where the number of interests is limited, for example, there is a greater chance of a 'rational' process of direct transfer, whereas, where the policy field is wider, with large numbers of actors involved, the need to accommodate different influences, interests and concentrations of power, may restrict the content of what is transferred and indeed the rationality of the transfer process.

An example of 'restricted policy transfer' in which only two countries were involved, the numbers of actors limited, and the policy at the heart of the transfer relatively circumscribed relates to the transfer of the Gateway Review Process for managing procurement processes from the U.K. to Australia (Fawcett and Marsh 2012). Fawcett and Marsh argue that key figures (in the state of Victoria initially) identified a successful policy for managing procurement that they believed to be of benefit and, over a period of some years, worked with counterparts in the U.K. to effect the transfer. While, of course, complexities abounded, senior civil servants on both sides of the process acknowledged the elite nature of the transfer environment and that 'support from the higher echelons of government and the public service is crucial if an initiative of this sort is to be successful' (Fawcett and Marsh 2012, p. 177).

Where power is less concentrated and the prospective policy is more publicly 'visible' and potentially contentious, the actors involved will be both more numerous and diverse, with the inevitable implication of competing interests and increased complexity. This wider environment is likely to be less conducive to the wholesale transfer of policies or institutions and may instead favour the importation of ideas, knowledge and 'soft policy'. Depending on its origins, the impetus for transfer can either be championed or vetoed by core institutions of government – depending on the particular configurations of power and influence in various policy subsystems (True *et al.* 2007) – or either championed or contested by influential interests outside formal state structures. Much depends on the prevailing policy environment and the perceived urgency of the need to import new policies or ideas. Further, how the capacity to influence decision-making is configured and concentrated will also bear closely on outcomes. In contrast to the Gateway Review Process considered by Fawcett and Marsh, Newburn's (2010, p. 344) discussion of the transfer interest in the U.S. 'zero tolerance' criminal justice policies provides an insight into how difficult policy transfer can be in a situation where power is less concentrated and multiple interests compete for influence. Newburn acknowledges that international – and media – interest in zero tolerance policing in the 1990s had a certain symbolic effect in the U.K. to the point where 'some of the ideas associated with such developments 'do seem subsequently to have influenced British government policy'. When it comes to charting evidence of direct policy transfer, however, Newburn is sceptical, noting countervailing factors in the forms of 'significant variation in policing philosophies and styles … [and] the diverse histories as well as the institutional and cultural contexts within which policing is organised and undertaken'. These factors speak of a differentiated system populated by formal and informal networks and practices that, taken together, contribute to an environment characterized by low-power concentration and multiple sets of interests – an environment, in other words, that is likely to support a transfer politics distinguished by reliance on mutual learning and the voluntary adoption and testing of policies or ideas.

Clearly, it is not possible here to cover the full range of possibilities contained within this power paradigm. In principle, as observed, the paradigm relates almost exclusively to policy transfer within and among Western nations. Once inside the paradigm, there is a great deal of knowledge to be gained through the examination of different examples of transfer and the particular configurations of power and influence that they exhibit. However, despite its popularity among political scientists, it is hard to argue that the ideas and examples of transfer and learning associated with this paradigm exhaust the theoretical and empirical reach of policy transfer analysis. The increasingly global scope of policy transfer makes it essential to take account of the different ways in which power and influence are exercised – and in particular how inequalities of power mediate, and indeed dictate, policy outcomes.

4.2 *Power as weighted bargaining (PWB)*

This paradigm relates to processes that are largely exogenous to the transfer location and embrace agents that have sufficient power and influence to negotiate with national governments from positions of strength over the adoption of particular policies and programmes, or to promote ideas that can influence internal policymaking. Negotiations do not take place among equals – although putatively powerful institutions may not always be successful in achieving desired policy take-up. Key actors include global or regional organizations, in addition to powerful nation states, that have the capacity to influence national governments. Again, key epistemic communities and global policy chains can also influence domestic policy debates, as can actors within domestic bureaucracies and policy communities themselves. Much depends on the positions particular organizations occupy in the hierarchy of global and regional governance, and the specific issues involved. As Deacon (2014), O'Brien (2009) and many others have observed, there are numerous international organizations that exercise power and influence at global, regional and national levels – too many to take into account here. Nevertheless, it is possible to divide these bodies into two rough categories, recognizing, however, that there is a good deal of overlap between them (Orenstein 2009). First, bodies like the International Labour Organization (ILO), certain United Nations' member agencies, such as the UN General Assembly itself, and many regional organizations use their reputations and global positions to exert 'influence' largely through ideational argument and persuasion. Second, in addition to a capacity to use their strategic positions to 'persuade', organizations such as the WB, the IMF and the World Trade Organization (WTO), as key institutions of global economic governance, can in certain contexts exercise a coercive capacity to 'create, supervise and enforce rules' (O'Brien 2009, p. 169).

A range of examples helps to illustrate the nature of PWB. At the softer end of the spectrum, prevailing power balances within nation states and domestic cultures can mediate the impact of ideas and policy solutions that originate outside the transfer location. Lopreite's (2012) account of Argentinian resistance to 'travelling ideas' concerning gender policies and reproductive rights is a case in point. Although, in Lopreite's (2012, p. 121) opinion, 'transnationalized ideas had a significant impact in a country like

Argentina, with a long tradition of neglecting reproductive rights', the extent of the impact was mediated in a number of ways. For example, the financial crisis of 2001–2002 created an opportunity for new thinking about poverty reduction and the nature of the family, which allowed elements of Argentinian political culture to come to terms with global thinking and policy solutions about reproduction, gender and the role of the family. In this way, the new ideas that came out of the 1994 Cairo Conference on Population and Development – ideas broadly supported by a WB interested in how changing gender roles might contribute to poverty reduction – gained political ground in Argentina particularly among progressive NGOs. However, because proto-natalist and maternalist ideology remained powerful in Argentina, the outcome, which saw the introduction of a range of reproductive rights but in the context of the continuation of strict abortion laws, can be understood as the result of a 'double bargaining' process involving both global and local levels of power and influence. On the one hand, core components of Argentinian society had to acknowledge and accept policies that granted greater reproductive rights because of the increasing global influence of ideas that supported them. In addition, the need for WB support for poverty reduction in a time of crisis made it difficult to resist WB-approved policies. On the other hand, heated internal debates among Argentinian politicians, bureaucrats, policy networks and social movements stimulated by these exogenous pressures also played an important role in the final configuration of policy outcomes.

Lying between soft and harder versions of PWB, the regional level in particular offers examples of learning and transfer that are par excellence 'bargained' solutions. As Yeates (2005, p. 6) has argued, because 'regional formations often entail groups of countries with similar cultural, legal and political characteristics, agreement on the scope and nature of transnational collaboration is more feasible'. Such agreement in turn provides opportunities for policy transfer because, 'processes of regional integration can create greater awareness of a range of common issues [and] contribute to the forging of transnational political alliances' (Yeates 2005, p. 7), the point being that smaller countries in particular can not only increase their bargaining position through membership of regional blocs but can also adopt (or mimic) policies used by other member states. Negotiation and bargaining are the hallmarks of policy transfer in the regional universe because regional formations do not generally possess powers of enforcement – the consequence being that notice has to be taken of the views of member states even though formal power structures are weighted against any one national government.

The European Union's (EU) Open Method of Coordination (OMC), which emerged from the European Employment Strategy (EES) in the late 1990s is a case in point. While this mechanism for EU-wide policy development is arguably less significant than it was, largely because its soft law approach has been overtaken by the more immediate requirement to 'support' the single market and monetary union in ways that are far from 'soft' or consensual (Hay and Wincott 2012, Papadopoulos and Roumpakis 2015), the OMC/EES stands as an attempt to encourage member states in a regional bloc to develop specific national policies benchmarked against collectively agreed objectives. The overall aim is to diffuse best practice through a process of mutual adjustment monitored at supranational level but underpinned by peer pressure to achieve the set targets (Schmidt and Radaelli 2004). Although it predated the OMC, the EES remains the best instance of how the process worked, with member states like France acknowledging the specific benefits they derived from learning about other member states' active labour market policies (Teague 2001; Trubeck and Mosher 2003, p. 44). Again, Radaelli (quoted in Guillén and Palier 2004, p. 204) has pointed to significance of 'cognitive harmonization' – 'the shaping and reshaping of perceptions of attitudes towards social problems and the way to tackle them'. The catch, of course, in this example of regional bargaining – and the inherent trickiness of determining the balance of the 'weight' in processes of weighted bargaining more generally – is that the overall OMC process became infused with a neo-liberal economic logic supported by the EU's main institutions that undoubtedly constrained the efforts of some national governments to pursue social democratic policy solutions (Radaelli 2003).

A different example of PWB comes in the form of the global bargaining processes that contributed to the creation of the UN's Millennium Development Goals (MDGs) during the 1990s. Fukuda-Parr *et al.* (2014, p. 107) describe how the UN's Millennium Declaration of 2000 that was agreed among the UN, the WB, the IMF, the OECD, and national governments, resulted from 'a decade of efforts to redefine the development agenda' involving organizations ranging from national governments to development agencies, policy networks and lobby groups. Key moments in the development of ideas involved a number of UN conferences such as International World Summit for Children in 1990, the 1994 Cairo conference on Population and Development and the Fourth World Conference on Women in Beijing in 1995, each of which influenced progress towards a global human rights agenda and, by implication, countered dominant neo-liberal ideas about the importance of the free market in economic development (Fukuda-Parr *et al.* 2014). However, although these processes were clearly influential in drawing attention to global inequalities and particularly the plight of women in developing economies, the MDGs themselves ultimately did not reflect the broader ambitions of the wide range of actors who had contributed to these debates. This failure of vision owed much to the fact that, despite their endorsement of the Millennium Declaration, the U.S. government, the WB, the IMF and the OECD pressured the UN to narrow its 'broader, more essentialist rights-based approach' (Saith 2006, p. 1170) in favour of the constrained, target-driven MDGs that these organizations preferred.

Of course, this demonstration of the power of these international institutions needs to be balanced against the willingness of national governments to implement the domestic policy changes required to meet the MDGs. Despite the apparent power of key global organizations, nations can often exercise a power of their own through their ability to choose both their level of commitment to external demands and standards, and how they interpret these demands. In the case of the MDGs, national governments were able to customize targets better to accord with their perceived needs (Sherematova undated) or present data in ways that demonstrated apparent conformity to core objectives such as poverty reduction despite significant regional variations (see, e.g. IMF 2004).

Elsewhere, this residual power that sovereign states can deploy to resist the logic of global institutions' policy demands can be seen in the apparently more 'coercive' instance of global anti-money laundering measures. The account of the role and influence of the Financial Action Task Force (FATF) provided by Hameiri and Jones (2016) makes it clear that well-positioned organizations, even if they cannot formally compel compliance under international law, can nevertheless deploy various techniques to 'encourage' the adoption of preferred policy solutions. In the case of FATF, the maintenance of a list of nations that were reluctant to implement various anti-money laundering policies demanded by the G7 group of countries contributed to a high degree of formal compliance, the fear being that failure to develop domestic Financial Intelligence Units and other state institutions to support international regulatory standards, would result in exclusion from global capital flows (Hameiri and Jones 2016, p. 11). Importantly, however, as Hameiri and Jones point out, the balance of power relations within national governments can either facilitate or undermine the enthusiasm with which externally created policy demands are pursued. In this case, internal bargaining about the desired strength of domestic regulatory institutions played a role in the configuration of the institutions themselves, the outcome being that these internal deliberations fed back into the external 'bargained environment', with global institutions having to accept that national compliance with many of their demands is likely to vary.

4.3 *Power as coercion*

'Coercion' can come in a range of different forms, some of which will inevitably lean towards the PWB paradigm, even as others display a clearly coercive character. If instances of simple 'policy imposition' are rare, there are many examples of 'transfer' where the conditions associated with a reluctance to adopt recommended policies are such as to leave a government with little choice but to implement them. A clear example of this dynamic comes in the form of the 'bailout' agreements imposed on Greece and other Southern European countries 'that were accompanied by the demand on behalf of the surplus countries … to implement far-reaching austerity reforms and reduce drastically social protection' (Papadopoulos and Roumpakis 2015, p. 195). These reforms were promoted by the European Council, the European Central Bank and the IMF, and were implemented alongside a number of other measures, such as the formal monitoring of wage and collective bargaining agreements, that resulted in a reduction in the ability of Greece (and indeed other debtor member states) to manage its own wage and budget-setting strategies (Papadopoulos and Roumpakis 2015, p. 196).

This sort of 'coercive conditionality' can also be observed in other areas of European social policy such as pension privatization. Orenstein (2008, 2013) has examined the spread of market-driven pensions reforms rooted in the ideas of the IMF and WB, and, to be sure, the character of discussions between these global organizations, other relevant players and national governments varies depending on the relative position of the country in question. With reference to Greece, Güleç (2014, p. 82) has pointed out that pressure for pension reform emerged partly because of exogenous pressures from the IMF and WB, and partly, too, as a result of 'the conditionality of (European) economic integration as a disciplinary form of adjustment' designed, *inter alia*, to control public spending. Of course, as many commentators have noted (see Hay and Wincott 2012), the EU's commitment to an inclusive European Social Model organized on social democratic lines has itself been compromised by an increasing attachment to the market liberal ideas and policies promoted by the OECD, WB and IMF – particularly in the wake of European enlargement.

Outside the EU, Ozkan's exploration of the roles of the WB, IMF and ILO in the development of Turkey's Unemployment Insurance (UI) scheme in the 1990s further illustrates the complexity of a process that involved a combination of external pressures to adopt particular measures and subsequent endogenous debate about their utility among a range of interests in Turkey itself. As Ozkan (2013, pp. 242–243) argues, 'the new UI programme in Turkey can be viewed as a foreign model conveyed by the World Bank and the Turkish economic bureaucracy and inspired by the liberal ideas of the OECD and the World Bank'. However, while the neo-liberal ideas of the WB and IMF 'actively played an important role in bringing the UI idea into the Turkish context' (Ozkan 2013, p. 246), debates among various Turkish advocacy coalitions helped to counter the initial preferences of employers and trade unions to maintain their traditional approach to unemployment based on early retirement options and generous statutory severance packages. The conversion of the Turkish civil service to market liberal ideas, supported by the WB and IMF, was clearly an important aspect of this 'translation' process.

Whether or not this example is a clear illustration of PC may appear debateable. After all, internal discussion clearly played a role in the introduction of UI in Turkey and this endogenous dynamic counters the impression that a policy had simply been imposed from without. However, when weighing up the relative power positions of contributing actors, it is important to take account of a context that is characterized by the ability of powerful international organizations both to set the ideational agenda and to create economic and financial incentives to 'encourage' compliance. In the Turkish case, internal debates were plainly influenced by the neo-liberal assumptions promoted by WB and IMF, and, in addition, both organizations were deeply involved in Turkey's economic fortunes by virtue of their contribution to the country's structural adjustment policies. In this way – and unlike the example of the FATF above – the transfer context was not conducive to a systematic defence of existing arrangements for unemployment provision.

A final – and different – instance of coercive transfer relates to the increasing role of public–private sector collaborations as champions and 'implementers' of particular policies. Holden examines the role of the U.K.'s Department of Health and the British healthcare industry in the export of the private–public partnership (PPP) and the private finance initiative (PFI) models to other countries. PPP/PFI effectively offers a means of using private capital to finance large public sector infrastructure projects, which are then leased to the public sector (usually) on a 20–30-year contract – an arrangement that guarantees a long-term income stream for the corporations involved. Holden (2009, p. 318) notes in relation to health infrastructure spending, that 'the adoption of PPPs by other countries is of particular strategic importance to British firms, since these are already market leaders in PPP due to its extensive use in the NHS'. The 'coercive' element in this instance of PPP/PFI export comes in the form of a government's decision to work with private healthcare firms to target a range of countries – usually developing economies – in order to 'sell' their expertise in the design, management and monitoring of PFI projects. As Holden (2009, p. 329) points out, because many countries, including large economies such as China's, lack expertise and know-how in managing PPP/PFI arrangements, there is a danger that 'a self-reinforcing process' is created 'in which greater private sector involvement is always seen as beneficial', despite the well-documented risks and drawbacks associated with PPP/PFI. It is possible, then, for countries to find themselves contractually bound into costly infrastructure projects on the basis of advice that is not impartial and where they share an undue burden of risk.

5. Conclusion

Having discussed the inherent difficulties that efforts to produce a theoretically plausible and methodologically sound model of policy transfer, open to empirical validation, encounter, this article has argued that it is more fruitful to use the insights developed in the policy transfer literature as independent variables capable of illuminating different components of policy analysis. The current discussion has concentrated on how an examination of the parameters of policy transfer can shed light on configurations of power in global policymaking – an area that has become increasingly important in recent years. Figure 1 provides a basic depiction of the key elements of the power–policy transfer relationship discussed in the article. Clearly this attempt to illustrate the various factors and relationships involved is schematic, and much more needs to be done by way of greater empirical detail – most obviously through more thorough case-study material – than the brief, indicative examples provided here. In closing, it is important to reiterate the ideal–typical character of the model and to acknowledge, once again, the innate complexities of this area of analysis. For example, the relative simplicity of the model as currently configured, although stressing the dynamic nature of relationships within Paradigms 1 and 2 (and arguably within Paradigm 3 but to a *much* lesser extent), means that it does not take adequate account of the possibility that different actors – particularly national

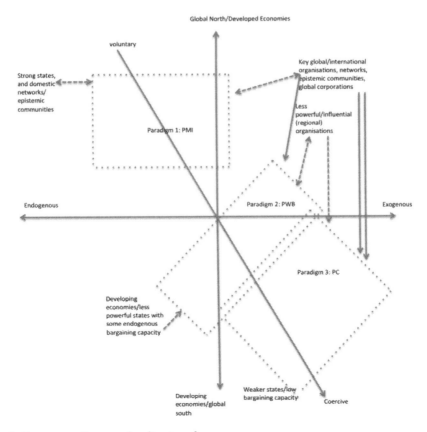

Figure 1. Power paradigms and policy transfer.

governments – could find themselves in *different* power relationships with key global and regional players depending on the particular policy issues and balance of forces, endogenous and exogenous, involved. This area – the extent to which power is differentially fractured according to the key policy issues and wider socio-economic context of specific policy debates – in particular would benefit from further investigation.

Note

1. The term 'policy transfer' is used as a shorthand to refer to a variety of types of policy movements including not only 'lesson-drawing' and 'policy learning', and other essentially 'mutual' forms of transfer but also the forms of bargained and conditional/coercive transfer that are characterized by the less equal power relationships contained in the second and third power paradigms discussed in the article.

Disclosure statement

No potential conflict of interest was reported by the author.

References

Adam, S. and Kriesi, H., 2007. The network approach. In: P. Sabatier, ed. *Theories of the policy process*. Cambridge, MA: Westview Press.

Béland, D., 2005. Ideas and social policy: an institutionalist perspective. *Social Policy and Administration*, 39 (1), 1–18. doi:10.1111/j.1467-9515.2005.00421.x

Benson, D. and Jordan, A., 2011. What have we learned from policy transfer research? Dolowitz and Marsh revisited. *Political Studies Review*, 9, 366–378. doi:10.1111/psr.2011.9.issue-3

Cebulla, A., 2005. 'The road to Britain's New Deal'. In: A. Cebulla, K. Ashworth, D. Green and R. Walker, eds. *Welfare-to-work: new labour and the US experience*. Aldershot: Ashgate.

Crozier, M., 2008. Listening, learning, steering: new governance, communication and interactive policy formation. *Policy & Politics*, 36 (1), 3–19. doi:10.1332/030557308783431616

Daguerre, A., 2007. *Active labour market policies and welfare reform: Europe and the US in comparative perspective*. Basingstoke: Palgrave. doi:10.1057/9780230582231

Daguerre, A. and Taylor-Gooby, P., 2004. Neglecting Europe: explaining the predominance of American ideas in new labour's employment policies since 1997. *Journal of European Social Policy*, 14 (1), 25–39. doi:10.1177/0958928704039786

Deacon, A., 2000. Learning from the USA? the influence of American ideas upon 'new labour' thinking on welfare reform. *Policy and Politics*, 28 (1), 5–18. doi:10.1332/0305573002500794

Deacon, B., 2014. Global and regional governance. In: N. Yeates, ed. *Understanding global social policy*. 2nd ed. Bristol: Policy Press.

Dolowitz, D. and Marsh, D., 1996. Who learns what from whom: A review of the policy transfer literature. *Political Studies*, 44, 343–357. doi:10.1111/j.1467-9248.1996.tb00334.x

Dolowitz, D. and Marsh, D., 2000. Learning from abroad: the role of policy transfer in contemporary policy making. *International Journal of Policy and Administration*, 13 (1), 5–23. doi:10.1111/gove.2000.13.issue-1

Dunlop, C. and Radaelli, C., 2013. Systematising policy learning: from monolith to dimensions. *Political Studies*, 61, 599–619. doi:10.1111/post.2013.61.issue-3

Dwyer, P. and Ellison, N., 2009. "We nicked stuff from all over the place": policy transfer or muddling through? *Policy & Politics*, 37 (3), 389–407. doi:10.1332/030557309X435862

Evans, M., 2009. Policy transfer in critical perspective. *Policy Studies*, 30 (3), 237–241. doi:10.1080/01442870902863810

Evans, M. and Davies, J., 1999. Understanding policy transfer: a multi-level, multi-disciplinary perspective. *Public Administration*, 77 (2), 361–385. doi:10.1111/padm.1999.77.issue-2

Evans, M., 2010. In conclusion. In: M. Evans, ed. *New directions in the study of policy transfer*. London: Routledge.

Farrell, M., 2009. EU policy towards other regions: policy learning in the external promotion of regional integration. *Journal of European Public Policy*, 16 (8), 1165-1184. doi:10.1080/13501760903332688

Fawcett, P. and Marsh, D., 2012. Policy transfer and policy success: the case of the gateway review process (2001–10). *Government and Opposition*, 47 (2), 162–185. doi:10.1111/j.1477-7053.2011.01358.x

Fukuda-Parr, S., Yamin, A., and Greenstein, J., 2014. The power of numbers: a critical review of millennium development goal targets for human development and human rights. *Journal of Human Development and Capabilities*, 15 (2–3), 105–117. doi:10.1080/19452829.2013.864622

Gallie, W., 1956. Essentially contested concepts. *Proceedings of the Aristotelian Society*, 56, 167–198. doi:10.1093/aristotelian/56.1.167

Guillén, A.M. and Palier, B., 2004. Introduction: does Europe matter? Accession to EU and social policy developments in recent and new member states. *Journal of European Social Policy*, 14 (3), 203–209. doi:10.1177/0958928704044619

Güleç, A., 2014. The politics of pension reform in Greece and Turkey: international institutions as external determinants of adjustments. *Global Social Policy*, 14 (1), 72–90. doi:10.1177/1468018113514866

Hameiri, S. and Jones, L., 2016. Global governance as state transformation. *Political Studies*, 64 (4), 793–810.

Hay, C. and Wincott, D., 2012. *The political economy of European capitalism*. Basingstoke: Palgrave.

Holden, C., 2009. Exporting public-private partnerships in healthcare: export strategy and policy transfer. *Policy Studies*, 30 (3), 313–332. doi:10.1080/01442870902863885

Holzinger, K. and Knill, C., 2005. Causes and conditions of cross-national policy convergence. *Journal of European Public Policy*, 12 (5), 775–796. doi:10.1080/13501760500161357

Hudson, J. and Lowe, S., 2009. *Understanding the policy process: analysing welfare policy and practice*. 2nd ed. Bristol: Policy Press.

International Monetary Fund/World Bank. 2004. Draft Global Monitoring Report, 2004. Unpublished.

Knill, C., 2005. Introduction: cross-national policy convergence: concepts, approaches and explanatory factors. *Journal of European Public Policy*, 12 (5), 764–774. doi:10.1080/13501760500161332

Lindblom, C. E., 1959. The science of "muddling through". *Public Administration Review*, 19 (2), 79–88. doi:10.2307/973677

Lindblom, C. E., 1979. Still muddling, not yet through. *Public Administration Review*, 39 (6), 517–526. doi:10.2307/976178

Lopreite, D., 2012. Travelling ideas and domestic policy change: the transnational politics of reproductive rights/health in Argentina. *Global Social Policy*, 12 (2), 109–128. doi:10.1177/1468018112443685

Lukes, S., 1974. *Power: a radical view*. Basingstoke: Macmillan.

Mahon, R., 2010. After neo-liberalism?: The OECD, the World Bank and the child. *Global Social Policy*, 10 (2), 172–192. doi:10.1177/1468018110366615

Marsh, D. and Evans, M., 2012. Conclusion: policy transfer into the future. *Policy Studies*, 33 (6), 587–591.

Massey, A., 2009. Policy mimesis in the context of global governance. *Policy Studies*, 30 (3), 383–395. doi:10.1080/01442870902888940

Newburn, T., 2010. Diffusion, differentiation and resistance in comparative penality. *Criminology and Criminal Justice*, 10 (4), 341–352. doi:10.1177/1748895810382381

O'Brien, R., 2009. Organizational politics, multilateral economic organizations and social policy. In: N. Yeates and C. Holden, eds. *The global social policy reader*. Bristol: Policy Press.

Orenstein, M., 2008. *Privatizing pensions: the transnational campaign for social security reform*. Princeton: Princeton University Press.

Orenstein, M., 2013. Pension privatization: evolution of a paradigm. *Governance*, 26 (2), 259–281. doi:10.1111/gove.2013.26.issue-2

Orenstein, M., 2009. Analysing transnational policy formation: the case of pensions privatization. In: N. Yeates and C. Holden, eds. *The global social policy reader*. Bristol: Policy Press.

Ozkan, U., 2013. Translating travelling ideas: the introduction of unemployment insurance in Turkey. *Global Social Policy*, 13 (3), 239–260. doi:10.1177/1468018113499575

Papadopoulos, T. and Roumpakis, A., 2015. Democracy, austerity and crisis: Southern Europe and the decline of the European Social Model. In: S. Romano and G. Punziano, eds. *The European social model adrift: Europe, social cohesion and the economic crisis*. Aldershot: Ashgate.

Radaelli, C., 2003. *The open method of coordination: a new governance structure for the European Union*. Stockholm: Swedish Institute for European Policy Studies, Report 1.

Rose, R., 1991. What is lesson-drawing? *Journal of Public Policy*, 11 (1), 3–30. doi:10.1017/S0143814X00004918

Saith, A., 2006. From universal values to millennium development goals: lost in translation. *Development and Change*, 37 (6), 1167–1199. doi:10.1111/j.1467-7660.2006.00518.x

Schmidt, V. and Radaelli, C., 2004. Policy change and discourse in Europe: conceptual and methodological issues. *West European Politics*, 27 (2), 183–210. doi:10.1080/0140238042000214874

Sheremotova, O., undated. *Acheving the MDGs; The Russian Federation, Global University Network for Innovation*. Available from: http://www.guninetwork.org/articles/achieving-millennium-development-goals-russian-federation [Accessed 2 May 2016].

Simmons, B. and Elkins, Z., 2004. The globalization of liberalization: policy diffusion in the international political economy. *American Political Science Review*, 98 (1), 171–189. doi:10.1017/S0003055404001078

Stone, D., 1999. Learning lessons and transferring policy across time, space and disciplines. *Politics*, 19 (1), 51–59. doi:10.1111/1467-9256.00086

Stone, D., 2004. Transfer agents and global networks in the "transnationalization" of policy. *Journal of European Public Policy*, 11 (3), 545–566. doi:10.1080/13501760410001694291

Stone, D., 2010. Private philanthropy or policy transfer? The transnational norms of the Open Society Institute. *Policy & Politics*, 38 (2), 269–287. doi:10.1332/030557309X458416

Stone, D., 2012. Transfer and translation of policy. *Policy Studies*, 33 (6), 483–499. doi:10.1080/01442872.2012.695933

Teague, P., 2001. Deliberative governance and EU social policy. *European Journal of Industrial Relations*, 7 (1), 7–26. doi:10.1177/095968010171002

Trubeck, D.M. and Mosher, J.S., 2003. New governance, employment policy and the european model. In: J. Zeitlin and D.M. Trubeck, eds. *Governing work and welfare in a new economy: European and American experiments*. Oxford: Oxford University Press.

True, J., Jones, B., and Baumgartner, F., 2007. Punctuated-equilibrium theory: explaining stability and change in public policy-making. In: P. Sabatier, ed. *Theories of the policy process*. 2nd ed. Cambridge, MA: Westview Press.

Yeates, N., 2005. *"Globalization" and social policy in a development context*. Geneva: United Nations Research Institute for Development, Social Policy Development Programme Paper 18.

RESEARCH ARTICLE

Social policy diffusion in South Asia

Joachim Betz and Daniel Neff

ABSTRACT
South Asia has seen the almost simultaneous introduction of contribution-free social schemes in employment, health, education and pensions which are often strengthened by constitutional amendments and the right to information about government acts and procedures for normal citizens. Given the diverging economic, political and social composition of the countries of the region the near simultaneous introduction of the rights-based cash transfer programmes might be attributed to regional policy diffusion, caused either by some common pressures, learning from neighbours, or emulation. Using the case of employment guarantee programmes we contribute to the diffusion literature by showing that the schemes were not copied fully, but adapted to the national social, political and financial circumstances of the countries, built on the respective programme predecessors or not copied at all. Governments in the region were able to choose not only the timing of introduction but also the scope, coverage and generosity as well as their regulatory framework for programme execution and monitoring. We argue that programme adoption is more likely if the programmes in question are compatible with the ideological leanings of the government, fit with the international social practice and compatible with already existing schemes. However, some similarities between the employment programmes in South Asia could be the result of the influence of external development actors with the result that former rather different programmes become alike.

1. Introduction

Since 1990, social transfer schemes with a guarantee-like, contribution-free and universal character have been introduced in more than 30 developing countries, an advance often characterized as a kind of quiet revolution (ILO 2010, Barrientos 2013). As causes and triggers of this revolution the lost decade in Latin America, the negative social effects of economic adjustment, widespread democratization in the developing world, growing tax income in emerging economies and the deficits of traditional social insurance programmes are most often advanced, while also pointing to the impact of some kind of global or regional contagion or diffusion effect. South Asia has been a laggard with regard to public social spending and introducing the new social protection schemes, but has made great advances during the last decade and half to join the front runners with new, mostly contribution-free social schemes in employment, health, education and pensions, which are often strengthened by constitutional amendments and the right to information about government acts and procedures for normal citizens. As economic development differs between the countries of the region, as well as public spending and income, the timing and scope of democratization and the political affiliation of the respective governments, the near simultaneous introduction of the rights-based cash transfer programmes might be attributed to regional policy diffusion, caused either by some common pressures, learning from neighbours, or emulation.

The simple coincidence of programme initiation in different countries, which is quite often taken as a sufficient proof of policy diffusion (e.g. Simmons and Elkins 2004, Brooks 2005, Weyland 2005, Swank 2006, Holden 2009, Sugiyama 2011, Brooks and Kurtz 2012, Gandrud 2013, Aklin and Urpelainen 2014) does, however, not tell the full story. New social schemes in South Asia were not copied fully by neighbours, but adapted to the national social, political and financial circumstances of the countries in question built on the respective programme predecessors or not copied at all (Pakistan). This also means that pressures for full-scale emulation or learning are less than often made out; governments in the region were free to choose not only the timing of introduction but also the scope, coverage and generosity as well as their regulatory framework for programme execution and monitoring. With regard to the causes for learning by neighbours, we argue that the expected political benefits seem to be the least analysed factor. Programme adoption is also more likely if the programmes in question are compatible with the ideological leanings of the government, fit with the international social practice and compatible with already existing schemes.

In the first part of the paper, we will deal with the social background of new social protection schemes globally. In the second part, we aim to explore the channels for diffusion and the underlying reasons for the almost simultaneous adoption of employment programmes with a rights-based character in South Asia and the extent to which they were copied.

2. Widening income inequality and the new social protection paradigm

Income inequality significantly increased during the last two decades in quite a few emerging economies. South Asia is no exception to this general rule. The growth elasticity of poverty (measuring the per cent change in poverty for a 1% change in mean income per capita) in South Asia has remained much lower compared with Southeast and East Asia between 1995 and 2010 (Hasan et al. 2009) and has thus been less inclusive. As a consequence SA has some of the worst levels of human deprivation in the world (ADB 2012a, 2012b, World Bank 2015). Moreover, national and subnational inequality has risen (in India, Nepal, Pakistan and Sri Lanka) or at least remained stagnant (Bangladesh) over time across the region (Rama et al. 2015).

Internationally, a change in the perception of the linkage between inequality and economic/social progress can be observed. Persistent inequality has been shown in quite a few recent studies as having not only no necessary connection with growth but also seems empirically strongly associated with *less sustained* growth (Berg and Ostry 2011), macroeconomic instability, more intense redistributive struggles, systematic exclusion of social groups and therefore lower trust among citizens, violence and conflicts (Zhuang *et al.* 2014; Rama *et al.* 2015). Inclusive growth has therefore become the blueprint for nearly all development-oriented International Organizations and of late – to all South Asian governments.

An important instrument to further inclusion is social assistance/protection for those who cannot compete on the market and/or are not covered by social insurance schemes. Since around 2000, social protection has emerged as a new paradigm for antipoverty thinking in the global South from conventional approaches of food aid, subsidies and other forms of 'safety nets' to regular and predictable forms of social assistance (Barrientos and Nino-Zarazúa 2011). A second noteworthy development was to base social protection schemes on a human rights approach (World Bank 2008). By this, citizens are empowered as 'rights-holders' citizens in relation to the state rather than merely as beneficiaries of social services. The 'rights-based approach' has become popular in South Asia too, because the scope of the informal sector did not decline despite strong economic growth, making the expansion of formal social security nearly impossible (Chakraborty 2010, Hujo and Cook 2012).

Three such universal schemes or rights-based programmes (employment, maternity and old-age pension schemes) have been introduced nearly simultaneously in India, Bangladesh and Nepal (but not in Pakistan) and were adapted to the respective circumstances. The aim of the paper is, therefore, to investigate the potential root causes of the diffusion, modification, or non-adoption employment programmes in South Asia. We thus try first to identify the most likely channels for diffusion using the case of employment schemes in South Asia. Second, we compare these programmes and show how similar they are and, if not, what the most prominent deviations from the blueprint set by the trendsetter are. Third, we aim to address the question why governments adapt social policy models from their neighbouring countries, and lastly, what the causal mechanisms are for the specific kind of policy diffusion.

3. Policy diffusion as a potential explanation of programme spread

The introduction of the new social cash-transfer programmes/minimum-income schemes with a rights-based character in South Asian countries could be a reflection of common socio-economic and political challenges (such as the ageing of the society, the erosion of family support, the progressive integration into the world market, the growing strength of the civil society, etc.), but we should note that the strength of these challenges differs significantly between South Asian countries. The spread of the programmes may therefore be due to some kind of policy diffusion.[1]

One example is the spread of universal or near-universal, non-contributory old-age pensions in the 1990s. Within South Asia, Nepal was the first to introduce such a programme on a national scale, which occurred in 1994 under the communist minority government and was followed by similar programmes (albeit with far smaller coverage) in India and Bangladesh in 1995 and 1998, respectively. A further innovation with a still very limited geographical spread comes in the form of tax-financed health insurance schemes for the poor or informally employed, who are insured against a predetermined set of treatments in hospital, provided by public or private institutions on a fixed basis. India was the front runner in this domain; Nepal, Bangladesh and Pakistan later introduced programmes for pregnant women (including cash incentives for pre and postnatal care).

Of late, some of the traditional employment programmes in South Asia were redesigned as rights-based schemes, providing a guaranteed minimum of labour supply, or, alternatively, the equivalent in financial unemployment compensation (Köhler 2011a, 2011b).

However, as shall be drawn out in the following, the diffusion of social protection schemes was not encompassing in South Asia as elsewhere, since programmes introduced by the respective front runner were never copied one-to-one but adapted to the special characteristics and political exigencies of the nations in question. Taken together these are indicators for policy diffusion (see also Köhler 2014, p. 35), but of an incomplete kind.

4. Channels for policy diffusion

The main channels for policy diffusion cited in the literature are coercion (by hegemonic states or international financial institutions), competition (for mobile capital), learning (from the experience of peer countries or epistemic communities) or emulation (of models regarded as appropriate and worth copying) (see e.g. Simmons et al. 2006, Dobbin et al. 2007). These channels are sometimes difficult to separate and may also add up.

Coercion should only play a minor role in diffusion of new programmes in South Asia. Hegemonic states outside the region have no real stake in them, and international financial institutions or bilateral agencies have only in Bangladesh co-financed schemes; the far greater burden was borne by the states of the region with little interference in the design from foreign agencies. Information on similar experiences elsewhere and expertise on their pros and cons provided by multilateral agencies may however have played a certain role. Similarly, competition cannot play a major role, as the integration of each country into the world economy is distinct (see for the general argument Burgoon 2001, Garrett and Mitchell 2001). In addition, beneficiaries of the new programmes introduced either have already retired from the market or are predominantly based in rural areas and do not export their production. Competition for mobile capital would have required not an expansion but more a restriction of social expenditures. This leaves us with learning and emulation as the remaining explanatory factors.

Learning occurs when actors gain new technical knowledge from the experience of others. Horizontal diffusion, that is, learning from neighbours in similar circumstances and/or with the same cultural background may offer appropriate models to copy (Brooks 2005). Problems with this approach are twofold: in the age of vastly expanding evidence on the proper set-up of social programmes (propagated by International Organizations) it is highly unlikely that governments need the experience of countries in the immediate neighbourhood to avoid costly mistakes. Second, it is necessary to clarify why governments should be eager to learn from or emulate other countries at all. Constructivism often passes over the political incentives to do so (see Simmons and Elkins 2004, Simmons et al. 2006, Dobbin et al. 2007, Linos 2011, Andrews et al. 2012, Cao 2012). They may comprise the eventual benefits (compared to status quo) of adopting them, the revealed effectiveness of programmes elsewhere, the ideological fit or proximity of the new programmes to the core values of the government in power, the partisan composition of the government, the structural legacy of earlier development strategies (path-dependency, given the shared colonial legacy) and – last but not least – the expected or realized electoral benefits of the initiatives (Meseguer and Gilardi 2009, Brooks and Kurtz 2012).

5. Differences and similarities between the national employment programmes

The **Indian** MGNREGS is the largest employment programme in the world and is purely tax-financed. It was first passed as an act in 2005 and then first introduced in 200 backward districts in early 2006 and subsequently implemented nationwide in 2008. Under the MGNREGS every rural household has the right to 100 days of guaranteed wage employment (in form of unskilled manual work) at a fixed wage rate within a year. The wage rates vary by state and are oriented at the minimum wage for the respective region but in reality often exceed the prevalent locally paid wage rates. Rural households have to be provided with work within 15 days of application otherwise they are eligible for unemployment allowance. This is an incentive for state governments to make an effort to provide households with paid work as they have pay for the unemployment allowance, as the MGNREGS wages are paid by the Centre. Similarly, the states have to compensate households in cases of delays in the payment of work undertaken. The MGNREGS is universal in its coverage as all (rural) households have a guaranteed right for 100 days of paid work. It is thereby self-targeting and demand driven, as the rural households have to actively seek work. Lastly, the MGNREGS is designed to be inclusive, as there are special provisions to allow socially excluded groups such as the so-called scheduled castes (SCs) or scheduled tribes (STs), women and elderly to take up work. Women are provided with child care facilities if they take up work and elderly have to work fewer hours and work is provided within 5 km of the homestead.

Following the Indian example, **Nepal** introduced a very similar tax-financed employment programme in 2006 referred to as the Karnali Employment Programme (KEP). The programme covers only five districts in the Karnali Zone (comprising only 1.3% of Nepal's population) in the Midwest, which is the most backward and remote area within Nepal and has experienced limited government support in the past (as it was a Maoist stronghold). But it covers the whole population of these districts, not only the poor (Government of Nepal 2012). Under the KEP – as with the MGNREGS – individuals in households who seek to do unskilled manual work are entitled to 100 days of paid employment at a fixed rate within a year. Households are only eligible, if none of their members either have a permanent or temporary employment in government or NGO or any income from a business (ILO 2010). Wages are fixed at district level and vary between Nepali Rs. 180–350 which lie below the district minimum wages. Similarly to the MGNREGA unemployment benefits are paid if no work is provided to the household (Government of Nepal 2012). The design of the programme is bottom-up as community user groups identify project areas and sites and households/individuals select themselves into the programme. KEP further aims to be inclusive as it tries to include all castes, but the integration of women and youth into the programme seem to leave a lot to be desired (Harris *et al.* 2013). Contrary to the Indian MGREGS KEP is not rights-based and despite its design has remained supply driven as only few projects were started in every district, resulting in the rationing of job offers and an average provision of only 18 days paid employment (KEPTA 2014). In recent years international agencies/donors and NGOs as well as the Nepali government have shown some interest in the implementation of a national employment guarantee scheme modelled after the Indian MGNREGA resulting in the commission of a employment guarantee bill in 2012 (by the National Planning Commission) which has however to date not (yet) been ratified due to the suspension of the Constituent Assembly.

A new programme similar to the MGNREGS in India was introduced in **Bangladesh** in 2008 as a response to the substantial price hike of essential commodities in connection with the global financial crisis (Government of Bangladesh 2010, Khuda 2011). After its initiation (100-Day Employment Generation Program – EGP) the programme and was subsequently modified, developed and renamed in 2009 (Employment Generation for the Hardcore Poor – EGHP) and 2010 (Employment Generation Programme for the Poorest – EGPP). The initial official objective was to create employment for the extreme poor who remain unemployed during the agricultural slack season amounting to up to 5 months during a year in order to strengthen their purchasing power and to help them escape poverty on the longer run. The EGPP has now become the largest social safety net programme in Bangladesh (Khuda 2011) since its introduction and has seen the largest rise in budget allocation in the last 2 years (World Bank 2014).

Contrary to the Indian model, Bangladesh's EGPP is neither rights-based, universal nor fully inclusive. It does not provide a statutory right (to work) but is merely a fiscal intervention by the government. Beneficiaries (households with less than half an acre of land and where the household head is a manual labourer) are identified at sub-district level by officials through a top-down process which is prone to corruption and inclusion and exclusion errors. The EGPP further only covers one (capable) adult member (aged 18–50) per household during two lean periods before harvest time – referred to as hunger seasons and after natural disasters within a year, whereas the MGNREGS covers all adult household members throughout the year (see also Zaman 2011, pp. 269–270) and only households which do not receive any other benefit from other social safety net programmes are eligible. Although now all rural areas are covered by the scheme, a special priority lies on the 81 most poverty-prone districts, mainly in the North and East of the country (Zaman 2011). Similarly to the MGNREGS the EGPP does guarantee an unemployment allowance (Tk. 40 per day for first 30 days and Tk.50/per day for 70 days), if no job is provided within 15 days after registration and it provides a fixed wage rate (at Tk. 100 per day, which amounts to approx. 1.3 US $), paid on a daily basis, which is however lower than the market wage levels for unskilled manual labour as to only attract those the most destitute (self-selection).

To summarize: by comparing the specificities of the respective employment programmes in India, Nepal and Bangladesh we could show that they significantly differ in major ways and hence were not copied 1:1. In contrast to India's MGNREGS Nepal's KEP is neither right-based, only regionally implemented, offers less than the minimum wage and is not fully inclusive. Similarly the Bangladesh EGPP is not fully identical to the MGNREGS: it is not rights-based, supply driven, offers less than the minimum wage and is also not fully inclusive. This clearly shows that the Bangladeshi and Nepali governments were free to choose not only the timing of introduction but also the scope, coverage and generosity as well as their regulatory framework for programme execution and monitoring.

6. Why should governments be eager to learn from neighbouring countries?

The expected political benefits of new social programmes are probably the least analysed factor of 'learning'. They seem to carry significant weight in South Asian democracies (and elsewhere). New governments have to choose on which programmes (among many candidates) to concentrate their limited means. In India, the nationwide employment programme was obviously a reaction to the industry-friendly course of the BJP government since 1998 and the introduction of a universal pension scheme in Nepal (an attempt of the left government to broaden its voter base). But expected electoral success does not explain everything: we thus hypothesize that contextual factors influence the adoption of policies and that programme ideas will only be taken up that (a) are compatible with the ideological leanings of the government in power (Gilardi et al. 2009), (b) fit with international/regional appropriate social practice. They are further more likely to finally implement a programme if (c) there is a possible linkage with existing social schemes and (d) the national/regional administration has the administrative and financial capacity to implement them.

That the MGNREGA was drafted and then subsequently came into being was the outcome of what Chopra (2011, 2014, p. 91), describes as an '[...] unusual process of consultation, negotiation and blurring of boundaries between state and non-state actors [...]' pre-2004 elections which saw the victory of the Congress-led coalition (United Progressive Alliance – UPA) – defeating the BJP led coalition (National Democratic Alliance – NDA) which failed to win over the largely rural electorate. The MGNREGA featured in the election party manifesto of the Indian National Congress (INC) in 2004 and is widely believed to have won the elections for the INC-led coalition. This victory – despite India's strong growth rate under the ruling BJP-led coalition ('India shining') – sent a strong signal to the region that political parties have to cater for their mainly rural electorate in order to succeed in elections. It was closely observed by the parties in the rather young democracies of the region. MGNREGA was not only discussed and appreciated by a multitude of India's civil society organizations – although most of them would have appreciated an even more generous scheme (Chopra 2014) – but was also fully compatible with the leanings of the Congress party – whose voter base had been since long a mixture of underprivileged minority groups and an urban intellectual elite – and their alliance partners.

It is open to debate if there was a strong popular demand in 'learning' countries to follow the example of the leaders. This would presuppose that voters are fully informed about the existence and merits of schemes initiated by leading countries (Linos 2011), most probably by newspaper articles. Our extensive Internet research in the archives of English medium newspapers in Nepal, Bangladesh and Pakistan has however not revealed a strong coverage either of the Indian MGNREGS in the other countries, nor many newspaper articles about their own employment programmes.

Bangladesh, despite its profound governance dysfunction, has become an exemplar of social development, overtaking India on many indicators such as health or education (Mahmud and Mahmud 2014). It is believed that this 'development surprise' (Mahmud et al. 2008) is a result of the political change from authoritarian to democratic rule in 1991 and the subsequent democratic elections. This, together with the influence of significant civil activism, a lively media, the strong presence of NGOs and the active foreign donor agencies, has led political parties to introduce and enhance welfare programmes in order to win elections and to please respective voter bases in their constituencies (Mahmud and Mahmud 2014, pp. 65–69). In its 2008 election Manifesto, the newly elected Awami League government put emphasis on poverty reduction through employment generation and subsequently implemented the employment guarantee programme after its victory (Khatun et al. 2010). In this context, the originally introduced employment programme (EGPP) was born fully out of own experiences to enhance self-targeting, introduce quota for women, community consultation, better guidelines, grievance redressal and awareness raising.

With the introduction of a multi-party democracy in the 1990s **Nepal** has seen the introduction of a number of social policy programmes. Currently, Nepal still finds itself in a phase of politically and socially fragile post-conflict situation and the recent devastation earth quake has not helped to improve the situation. The country is being characterized by a feudal social order, with a large population facing food insecurity and exclusion on the basis of caste, ethnicity, gender, language and geography (Khatiwada and Köhler 2014). Following the Comprehensive Peace Agreement (CPA) in 2006 – which brought an end to a decade of civil war (1996–2006) – and the formulation of an interim constitution in 2007 the current government focus lies on reconstruction and post-conflict development, with a special focus on social protection and social inclusion in order to build legitimacy and to secure popular support (Khatiwada and Köhler 2014). The introduction of the KEP is seen as the response to the pressure of an active Karnali lobby group comprising political leaders and activists (Harris et al. 2013, p. 15) – introduced a number of programmes in the Karnali Zone (e.g. also the Child Development Grant), which is regarded as the poorest area in Nepal and has been a Maoist stronghold during the civil war. As laid out earlier, there is some serious interest by the Nepali government, the IDA and NGOs to introduce a national employment guarantee act and scheme modelled after the Indian MGNREGA which has resulted in the commission of a employment guarantee bill in 2012 (by the National Planning Commission) it has however to date not been ratified due to the unstable political conditions.

Pakistan's social expenditure on safety nets has for a long time the lowest in the region (e.g. World Bank 2007). From 2007 onwards, this has changed with the introduction of a National Social Protection Strategy in order to address persistent poverty and vulnerability. After the 2008 elections – which saw the defeat of the military rule of Pervez Musharraf and the victory of Pakistan People's Party (PPP) under the late Benazir Bhutto, which claimed to speak for the poor – the Benazir Income Support Programme (BISP) was introduced. Earlier programmes like the Bait-ul-Mal or Zakat were charity based and of limited coverage and impact. Social spending subsequently increased fivefold until 2012, but most resources were still spend for disparate, badly targeted subsidies, or weakly coordinated schemes of different agencies (World Bank 2013).

As laid out in the earlier sections of this paper, the new employment programmes are fully in line with international best practice and thinking. All International and Regional Organizations in the field did recommend the adoption of universal, contribution-free and rights-based social protection schemes for people in the informal sector or not covered by traditional social insurance at all and argued with their positive effects on poverty reduction, reduction of vulnerability income smoothing and affordability. This also led them to support the new programmes with programmatic, technical and (sometimes) financial assistance.

The employment programme in **Bangladesh** is supported by the World Bank since 2010. Its design has then benefited from the independent assessment and financial support of the World Bank (2010a). The Bank was especially asked to help to improve the governance of the programme and to prevent leakages. After its first years (2008–2010), when the programme was clientele-oriented and commonly known as the 'lazy allowance', the Bangladesh government was eager to use international experience and asked the International Development Assistance (IDA) to help in improvement. In this process a sizeable number of ghost workers were identified and it became apparent that the monitoring needed to be improved. Since 2013 the World Bank has committed for a second project (with a volume of 500 Mio. US$) to improve the functioning of all social programmes in Bangladesh. The experiences during the employment programme shall be used to gradually turn these into cash-based schemes (World Bank 2014).

The World Bank was similarly active in **Nepal** where it supported the installation of a safety net (with 21.7 Mio. US $) and specific safety net programmes – including employment programmes – with 45 Mio. US $ (World Bank 2010b). Similar employment programmes were also co-financed by the German GIZ on behalf of the World Food Programme. Lately, the government of Nepal has recently requested the UK Department for International Development (DFID) to help improve the KEP.

Despite financial support in some cases, international and national assistance agencies, the vast majority of new employment programmes were all initiated by the respective governments themselves and have remained overtly tax-financed. Yet, donor agencies had some influence on the (re)design and improvement of programmes, often based on the experiences made with MGNREGS. Diffusion in this context would thus imply that distinct employment programmes finally become alike because of similar suggestions by these agencies.

Employment programmes have a long history in South Asia, with a known early programme in Pakistan dating back as far as the 12th century (Subbarao *et al.* 2013, p. 3ff). Within modern South Asia many employment programmes were first established during British rule in order to deliver famine relief (Drèze 1990) and were expanded after independence in basically all former British colonies. However, in the last decade, with the introduction of the Mahatma Gandhi Rural Employment Guarantee Act (MGNREGA) in 2005 a new form of EPs has emerged.[2] This model has at least partially taken up by Bangladesh, Nepal but not Pakistan. In **Bangladesh** for example, the nationwide Employment Guarantee Programme for the Poorest drew on the Food for Work (1974) and Rural Maintenance Programmes (1983) – and replaced these with only minor adjustments (World Bank 2010c), but were at the same time also oriented towards the Indian MGNREGS.

Nepal on the other hand has added the regional KEP (in 2006) to its social protection programme portfolio supplementing the existing Rural Community Infrastructure Works (RCIW) Programme (in place since 1996). **Pakistan** in contrast, has implemented a cash for work programme (in refugee areas) as early as 1984.

Following the Indian model Pakistan also started to design an EP programme for rural unskilled workers entitling them to 100 days of paid work during a year at the minimum wage level. The employment programme was one of the election promises of the PPP in their election manifesto in 2008. A pilot scheme was introduced in 10 least developed districts in 2010, but the programme was then never implemented. After internal discussion within the government and bureaucracy the government concluded that it was not feasible to introduce a nationwide employment programme and thus finally introduced a direct cash transfer scheme (the BISP) in 2008 instead of the earlier proposed employment guarantee scheme (Gazdar 2014).

All South Asian countries display limited fiscal space for financing additional social schemes or enlarging them. Government revenues (as a percentage of GDP) are generally very low, compared to peer countries elsewhere, and lower in Pakistan, Nepal and Bangladesh as in India. In Bangladesh and Nepal there was a slight improvement in available fiscal space after 2009/10, in Pakistan practically not. In addition, all three countries suffer from a very limited debt space (internal and international borrowing). In addition, growth rates in Pakistan were much lower than in the rest of South Asia, due to political conflicts and instability (World Bank 2013). In Bangladesh, the initial employment programme (EGPP) promised 100 days of paid work, but due to a rise of the daily wages and subsequent financial shortages the work days guaranteed was reduced to 80 days. Similarly financial considerations play a major role why Nepal has – despite the political circumstances – not introduced a universal employment programme. The cost of such an expansion would be prohibitive and Nepal's limited public management capacity would make this difficult (Harris et al. 2013). Moreover the KEP, due to financial constraints, on average only provides households with 18 days of paid work (KEPTA 2014).

7. Conclusion

The literature on policy diffusion has mainly been preoccupied with analysing whether policy programmes have been adopted or not and when. Most studies do not differentiate to what *extent* programmes are taken up (geographically or socially) and do not analyse *which* components of the policies were not adopted and the reasons for non-adoption. Our study tries to fill this gap.

We did show that employment programmes with a rights-based character have indeed diffused within South Asia. But, we believe that common socio-economic challenges cannot fully explain this process horizontally. If so, programme design, coverage, generosity, programme governance and rights to employment provision should have been nearly identical, which they are not. Pakistan, with a very low level of social protection for the poor, should have adopted a similar scheme which it has not. Instead, it introduced an entirely different scheme with the Benazir Bhutto Income Support Programme. Moreover, neither Bangladesh nor Nepal based their employment programmes on a legal act as India, their schemes are thus not (yet) rights-based. These programmes also differ on a number of characteristics in relation to the Indian MGNREGS: they are less generous, less inclusive, only partly demand driven and chronically underfinanced. This is a clear sign that the government of the region were free to choose not only the timing of introduction but also the scope, coverage and generosity (this being partly determined by the restricted financial leeway) and the regulatory framework for programme execution and monitoring.

Second, we have tried to argue that there were some common motives for the introduction of new employment programmes in South Asia after 2005. As Andrews (2012) shows, crises are important triggers for reforms, although countries then implement them differently and at diverging time points. In South Asia, food insecurity and malnutrition, despite a multitude of schemes for alleviation, was prominent among them, as well as underemployment of agricultural labour in the slack season. Food insecurity raised in 2009/10 due to the rapid increase of staple food prices to a new height, exacerbated by a fall in remittance flows during the global financial crisis and natural disasters. But these problems are not of a recent character and got more severe *after* the initiation of the new schemes. Yet, traditional food for work or food subsidies absorbed a large and growing share of public expenditures in all South Asian countries, without much improving nutritional security of the poor, due to massive leakage to the wealthier groups, rotting of food and simple corruption. These programmes were characterized therefore by a very modest cost-benefit ratio and had reached a dead end, absorbing means which could have been directed to better use (for the improvement of social and physical infrastructure, etc.) more in line with making the countries fit for the world market, while simultaneously assisting the very poor. These problems, however, did persist for quite a while.

Third, the timing of reforms for the new employment programmes has much to do with political exigencies and developments. Employment programme has first been introduced by India in the context of the 2004 elections, where the Congress opposition attacked the government on their poor record of caring for the poor, while cultivating the industry, the cities and the upper classes. A scheme meant for the rural poor, certainly not a stronghold of the governing BJP and some of its alliance partners, was therefore most appropriate as an election topic. Its proposition tilted – according to quite a few observers – the balance significantly in favour of Congress. This success did certainly not get unnoticed by the governments of India's neighbours. In Nepal the KEP was introduced after the end of the civil war in 2006, bringing a 'Maoists' at the helm of the government. The Karnali region is a traditional Maoist stronghold. In favouring this region, the Maoists only followed the practice of the other Nepalese parties who all designed new social schemes targeted at particular regions. In Bangladesh, the start of the programme happened during a period of intensifying political struggle between the two dominant and rival parties (Awami League and BNP), displaying nearly identical electoral strength and therefore in need to broaden their base. Hence, the 100 days programme figured prominently in the 2008 election manifest of the Awami League (Khatun *et al.* 2010). In Pakistan, the introduction of a similar employment guarantee schemes was promised before elections by the PPP in 2008, but the government then soon realized that a direct cash transfer is more feasible and the BIP was introduced instead.

Fourth, some of the differences can also be explained by the available administrative capacities of the countries. In Pakistan, an earlier envisaged employment programme with a rights-based character was not introduced because of the opposition from bureaucracy who felt that they were not in the position to manage and monitor a national programme of such a scale. The differences in the administrative capacity of the South Asian countries are partly the result of missing precursor programmes to build upon. In contrast to India and Bangladesh, neither in Pakistan nor Nepal any national employment schemes have been in place earlier. Similarly, financial constraints were a limiting factor: neither Nepal nor Bangladesh was in a position to fully convert their schemes into a national scale.

Finally, we argued that the similarities between the employment programmes could partly be the result of the influence of external development actors (such as the World Bank or DFID) which have been asked to evaluate and improve the existing employment programmes which have been implemented rather ad hoc in Bangladesh and Nepal and thus lacked a proper structure and respective guidelines. These agents have then used the successful Indian example to provide suggestions on how to improve programmes. Through this process, former rather different programmes become alike, thus learning took place not at beginning, but at a later stage of programme implementation.

Notes

1. On diffusion and the causal mechanisms of its occurrence, the empirical evidence is meanwhile quite large; a number of studies have been published on privatization, liberalization and deregulation (Leisering 2004, Simmons and Elkins 2004, Simmons et al. 2006), pension reforms in Latin America (Brooks 2005, Levy and Schady 2013, Orenstein 2013), conditional cash transfers (also with a focus on Latin America; Hall 2008, Sugiyama 2011, Marzo and Mori 2012, Levy and Schady 2013) and on social cash transfers (Leisering 2009).
2. The predecessor of the MGNREGA in India was introduced in the state of Maharashtra (Maharashtra Employment Guarantee Scheme – MEGS) as a response to a severe drought in the 1970s and is generally seen as a great success (Pellissery 2006, Subbarao et al. 2013).

Disclosure statement

No potential conflict of interest was reported by the authors.

References

Asian Development Bank, 2012a. *Framework of inclusive growth indicators 2012. Key indicators for Asia and the Pacific*. Manila: ADB.

Asian Development Bank, 2012b. *Asian development outlook 2012. Confronting rising inequality in Asia*. Manila: ADB.

Andrews, C., et al., 2012. *Social protection in low income countries and fragile situations. Challenges and future directions*. Washington, DC: World Bank, Social Protection and Labor Discussion Paper, No. 1209.

Andrews, M., 2012. Developing countries will follow post-crisis OECD reforms but not passively this time. *Governance*, 25 (1), 103–127. doi:10.1111/gove.2012.25.issue-1

Aklin, M. and Urpelainen, J., 2014. The global spread of environmental ministries: domestic-international interactions. *International Studies Quarterly*, 58 (4), 764–780. doi:10.1111/isqu.2014.58.issue-4

Barrientos, A., 2013. *Social assistance in developing countries*. Cambridge: Cambridge University Press.

Barrientos, A. and Nino-Zarazúa, M., 2011. *Social transfers and chronic poverty. Objectives, design, reach and impact*. Manchester: Manchester University, Chronic Poverty Research Centre.

Berg, A. and Ostry, J., 2011. *Inequality and unsustainable growth: two sides of the same coin?* Washington D.C.: IMF Staff Discussion Note SDN/11/08.

Brooks, S., 2005. Interdependent and domestic foundations of policy change: the diffusion of pension privatization around the world. *International Studies Quarterly*, 49 (2), 273–294. doi:10.1111/isqu.2005.49.issue-2

Brooks, S. and Kurtz, M., 2012. Paths to financial policy diffusion: statist legacies in latin America's globalization. *International Organization*, 66 (1), 95–128. doi:10.1017/S0020818311000385

Burgoon, B., 2001. Globalization and welfare compensation: disentangling the ties that bind. *International Organization*, 55 (3), 509–551. doi:10.1162/00208180152507542

Cao, X., 2012. Global networks and domestic policy convergence: a network explanation of policy changes. *World Politics*, 64 (3), 375–425. doi:10.1017/S0043887112000081

Chakraborty, A., 2010. *Social protection policies in South Asia*. Paris: UNESCO.

Chopra, D., 2011. Interactions of 'power' in the making and shaping of social policy. *Contemporary South Asia*, 19 (2), 153–171. doi:10.1080/09584935.2011.565312

Chopra, D., 2014. The Mahatma Gandhi national rural employment guarantee act, India: examining pathways towards establishing rights-based social contracts. *The European Journal of Development Research*, 26 (3), 355–369. doi:10.1057/ejdr.2014.6

Dobbin, F., Simmons, B., and Garrett, G., 2007. The global diffusion of public policies: social construction, coercion, competition, or learning? *The Annual Review of Sociology*, 33 (1), 449–472. doi:10.1146/annurev.soc.33.090106.142507

Drèze, J., 1990. Famine prevention in India. *In*: J. Drèze and A. Sen, eds. *The political economy of hunger*. Vol. II. Oxford: Oxford University Press.

Gandrud, C., 2013. The diffusion of financial supervisory governance ideas. *Review of International Political Economy*, 20 (4), 881–916. doi:10.1080/09692290.2012.727362

Garrett, G. and Mitchell, D., 2001. Globalization, government spending and taxation in the OECD. *European Journal of Political Research*, 39 (2), 145–177. doi:10.1111/ejpr.2001.39.issue-2

Gazdar, H., 2014. Political economy of reform: social protection reform in Pakistan. *In*: G. Köhler and D. Chopra, eds. *Development and welfare policy in South Asia*. London: Routledge, 148–164.

Gilardi, F., Füglister, K., and Luyet, S., 2009. Learning from others: the diffusion of hospital financing reforms in OECD countries. *Comparative Political Studies*, 42 (4), 549–573. doi:10.1177/0010414008327428

Government of Nepal, 2012. *National planning commission*. Kathmandu, Nepal: Assessment of Karnali Employment Programme.

Government of the People's Republic of Bangladesh, 2010. *Employment Generation Program for the Poorest (EGPP), Environmental Management Framework (EMF)*. Dhaka: Ministry of Food and Disaster Managment.

Hall, A., 2008. Brazil's Bolsa família: a double-edged sword? *Development and Change*, 39 (5), 799–822. doi:10.1111/j.1467-7660.2008.00506.x

Harris, D., McCord, A., and Sony, K.C., 2013. *Politics of a national employment guarantee scheme in Nepal: an initial assessment of feasibility*. London: ODI.

Hasan, R., Magsombol, M., and Cain, J., 2009. *Poverty impact of the economic slowdown in developing Asia: some scenarios*. Manila: ADB, ADB Economics Working Paper Series No. 153.

Holden, C., 2009. Exporting public-private partnerships in health care: export strategy and policy transfer. *Policy Studies*, 30 (3), 313–332. doi:10.1080/01442870902863885

Hujo, K. and Cook, S., 2012. The political economy of social pension reform in Asia. *In*: S. Handayani and B. Babajanian, eds. *Social protection for older persons. Social pensions in Asia*. Manila: Asian Development Bank, 11–59.

International Labour Organisation, 2010. *Extending social security to all. A guide through challenges and options*. Geneva: ILO.

KEPTA, 2014. *Karnali employment programme technical assistance*. Kathmandu: Centre of Excellence Project Lessons Learned.

Khatiwada, Y. and Köhler, G., 2014. Political economy of reform: social protection reform in Pakistan. *In*: G. Köhler and D. Chopra, eds. *Development and welfare policy in South Asia*. London: Routledge, 129–147.

Khatun, F., Khan, T., and Nabi, A., 2010. *Employment generation for the hardcore poor and national service challenges of effective implementation*. Bangladesh: Centre for Policy Dialogue.

Khuda, B.-E., 2011. Social safety net programmes in Bangladesh: a review. *Bangladesh Development Studies*, 34 (2), 87–108.

Köhler, G., 2011a. *Social protection and socioeconomic security in Nepal*. Sussex: IDS Working Paper No. 370. doi:10.1111/j.2040-0209.2011.00370_2.x

Köhler, G., 2011b. Transformative social protection: reflections on South Asian policy experiences. *In: International conference: 'social protection for social justice'*, Sussex: IDS. doi:10.1111/j.1759-5436.2011.00280.x

Köhler, G., 2014. *The MDGs and social policy innovations from South Asia*. CROP Poverty Brief. Bergen: University of Bergen.

Leisering, L., 2004. *Social policy learning und Wissensdiffusion in einer globalisierten Welt*. Bielefeld: University of Bielefeld, Institute for World Society Studies, Social World – Working Paper no. 6.

Leisering, L., 2009. Extending social security to the excluded: are social cash transfers to the poor an appropriate way of fighting poverty in developing countries? *Global Social Policy*, 9 (2), 246–272. doi:10.1177/1468018109104628

Levy, S. and Schady, N., 2013. Latin America's social policy challenge: education, social insurance, redistribution. *Journal of Economic Perspectives*, 27 (2), 193–218. doi:10.1257/jep.27.2.193

Linos, K., 2011. Diffusion through democracy. *American Journal of Political Science*, 55 (3), 678–695. doi:10.1111/ajps.2011.55.issue-3

Mahmud, W., Ahmed, S., and Mahajan, S., 2008. Economic reforms, growth and governance: the political economy aspects of bangladesh's development surprise. *In*: D. Brady and M. Spencer, eds. *Leadership and growth*. Washington, DC: World Bank, 227–254.

Mahmud, S. and Mahmud, W., 2014. Development, welfare and governance: explaining Bangladesh`s 'development surprise'. *In*: G. Köhler and D. Chopra, eds. *Development and welfare policy in South Asia*. London: Routledge, 65–84.

Marzo, F. and Mori, H., 2012. *Crisis response in social protection*. Washington, DC: World Bank, Social Protection and Labor Discussion Paper, No. 1205.

Meseguer, C. and Gilardi, F., 2009. What is new in the study of policy diffusion? *Review of International Political Economy*, 16 (3), 527–543. doi:10.1080/09692290802409236

Orenstein, M., 2013. Pension privatization: evolution of a paradigm. *Governance*, 26 (2), 259–281. doi:10.1111/gove.2013.26.issue-2

Pellissery, S., 2006. *Do public works programmes ensure employment in the rural informal sector? Examining the employment guarantee scheme in rural Maharashtra, India*. Oxford: University of Oxford Working Paper, Department of Social Policy and Social Work, Barnett House.

Rama, M., et al., 2015. *Addressing inequality in South Asia. South Asia development matters*. Washington, DC: World Bank.

Simmons, B. and Elkins, Z., 2004. The globalization of liberalization: policy diffusion in the international political economy. *American Political Science Review*, 98 (1), 171–189. doi:10.1017/S0003055404001078

Simmons, B., Dobbin, F., and Garrett, G., 2006. Introduction: the international diffusion of liberalism. *International Organization*, 60 (4), 781–810. doi:10.1017/S0020818306060267

Subbarao, K., et al., 2013. *Public works as a safety net: design, evidence, and implementation*. Washington, DC: World Bank.

Sugiyama, N., 2011. The diffusion of conditional cash transfer programs in the Americas. *Global Social Policy*, 11 (2–3), 250–278. doi:10.1177/1468018111421295

Swank, D., 2006. Tax policy in an era of internationalization: explaining the spread of neoliberalism. *International Organization*, 60 (4), 847–882. doi:10.1017/S0020818306060280

Weyland, K., 2005. Theories of policy diffusion lessons from Latin American pension reform. *World Politics*, 57 (2), 262–295. doi:10.1353/wp.2005.0019

World Bank, 2007. *Social protection in Pakistan. Managing household risks and vulnerability*, Washington, DC: World Bank, Human Development Unit, South Asia Report No. 35472-PK.

World Bank, 2008. *Realizing rights through social guarantees: an analysis of new approaches to social policy in Latin America and South Africa*. Washington, D.C.: World Bank.

World Bank, 2010a. *Project appraisal document on a proposed credit for an employment generation program for the poorest project*, Washington, DC: World Bank, Report No. 52886-BD.

World Bank, 2010b. *Emergency project paper on an proposed additional credit to Nepal for a safety net project*. Washington, DC: World Bank.

World Bank, 2010c. *Bangladesh. Public expenditures and institutional review. Towards a better quality of public expenditure*. Washington, DC: World Bank.

World Bank, 2013. *Pakistan. Towards an integrated national safety net system*. Washington, DC: World Bank.

World Bank, 2014. *Implementation completion and results report on a credit to the people's republic of Bangladesh for an employment generation program for the poorest project*. Washington, DC: World Bank.

World Bank, 2015. *World bank poverty data - poverty rates in SA*. Available from: http://data.worldbank.org/topic/poverty [Accessed 10 September 2015].

Zaman, H., 2011. Assessing the impact of employment generation programs in challenging rural poverty: a comparative study on Bangladesh and India. *Journal of Poverty*, 15 (3), 259–276. doi:10.1080/10875549.2011.588303

Zhuang, J., Kanbur, R., and Rhee, C., 2014. *Rising inequality in Asia and policy implications*. Manila: Asian Development Bank Institute, Working Paper 463.

RESEARCH ARTICLE

India's emerging social policy paradigm: productive, protective or what?

Stefan Kühner and Keerty Nakray

ABSTRACT
This article presents a cross-disciplinary review of state-of-the-art explorations of India's emerging social policy paradigm during the two recent Centre/Left Congress/United Progressive Alliance (UPA) governments (2004–2009, 2009–2014). In doing so, it revises existing classifications of social policy activity in India by tracing quantitative inputs and outcomes over time and assessing the extension of social rights via newly introduced social policy programmes. We find little evidence that India has moved beyond its failing informal welfare regime features characterized by a weakly developed mix of productive–protective welfare policy interventions, comparatively low social expenditure and mixed social outcomes. Furthermore, testing the transformative character of social policy innovations, we conclude that India's approach to social protection has so far remained essentially residual, even minimalist, in character. Addressing the key developmental challenges India faces will therefore necessitate further reaching changes towards a more encompassing and inclusive social model that will in turn help to better generate productive assets among the Indian poor.

1. Introduction

Comparative social policy researchers have increasingly become interested in India. Estimated to overtake the Chinese total population in 2020 and to exceed it by around 400 million in 2050 (James 2011), India is regarded as a key contributor to regional economic growth – not least because of a substantial demographic dividend resulting from a shift in India's population age structure (Jones and Ramchand 2013; Rada and Von Arnim 2014). Yet, India's economic development has so far been at odds with China and other East Asian tiger economies, where increases in real GDP per capita have relied much more firmly on rapid productivity growth in manufacturing (Storm and Naastepad 2005). Around 65% of Indian employment remains committed to the low value-added agriculture sector, while manufacturing (predominantly focussed on construction) accounts for less than 10%. India's human capital is disproportionately concentrated in IT and IT-enabled services (Broadberry and Gupta 2010). The widening of the Indian domestic market is hampered by the very large share of informal employment – only

21% of working men (aged 15–59) had a regular salaried job in 2012, while only 13% of women had such employment (ILO 2014b) – and an agriculture sector that finds it increasingly challenging to sustain inflationary pressures due to rising real wages. There is today a vigorous debate in India about the role of redistribution and government profligacy within a political economy that emphasizes job creation and economic growth as a key prerequisite of poverty alleviation (Bhagwati and Dongardive 2013, Drèze and Sen 2013, Mazumdar 2014).

These trends and debates in India mirror a more general shift in the academic discourse on the sequencing of economic development and the role of social protection on the international stage (see Cook and Kabeer 2010, Surender and Walker 2013, Köhler and Chopra 2014). Several international organizations have stressed the need for 'more effective' social protection policies in the Global South (see e.g. ADB 2008, ILO 2011, 2014a; OECD 2011, UNDP 2014) and moved as far as acknowledging the pro-growth effects of distributional policy measures more generally (Balakrishnan *et al.* 2013, Bussolo and Lopez-Calva 2014, Ostry *et al.* 2014). While human capital investment has been advocated as a key priority to achieve the Millennium Development Goals (UN 2014), the United Nations Resolution on Sustainable Development (UN 2015) specifically aims to reduce inequalities of outcomes as well as to facilitate equality of opportunity. Indeed, governments in many Asian countries responded to the failure of existing safety nets to alleviate high inequality and chronic poverty in the context of global competition by increasing social protection efforts (Devereux and Sabates-Wheeler 2004).

A case in point are the two recent Centre/Left Indian governments of the Congress/United Progressive Alliance (Congress/UPA, 2004–2009; 2009–2014), which implemented a series of new social programmes giving India a 'regional leadership role' in social policy (Barrientos and Hulme 2009, p. 445). This article presents a cross-disciplinary review of state-of-the art attempts to explore in more detail, India's emerging social policy paradigm during these two incumbencies. In doing so, it revises existing classifications of social policy activity in India by tracing quantitative inputs and outcomes over time and assessing the extension of social rights via these newly introduced social policy programmes. We find little evidence that India has moved beyond its failing-informal welfare regime features characterized by a weakly developed mix of productive–protective welfare policy interventions, comparatively low social expenditure and mixed social outcomes (Wood and Gough 2006, Kühner 2015). Furthermore, using Koehler's (2011) framework for testing the transformative character of social policy innovations, we further conclude that India's approach to social protection has so far remained essentially residual, even minimalist, in character. Addressing the key developmental challenges India faces will therefore necessitate further reaching changes towards a more encompassing and inclusive social model that will in turn help to better generate productive assets among the Indian poor.

The article is structured as follows: we start with a review of existing conceptual classifications of the Indian welfare regime (Section 2). We then trace key social policy developments in India quantitatively (Section 3) before briefly introducing the new social programmes based on their protective–productive intent (Section 4). Our discussion of the extension of social rights and the transformative character of these new social programmes will follow (Section 5) and directly lead to our final conclusion (Section 6).

2. The Indian welfare regime in the literature

The 'welfare modelling business' outside of the rich EU and OECD countries has been directly influenced by debates in Western comparative welfare research. At the same time, there have also been numerous parallel attempts to emphasize the unique processes of welfare state development in East and Southeast Asia. India has not yet been dealt with very systematically in this literature. This article was conceived on the back of two recent attempts to more systematically capture the Indian welfare regime in comparative perspective.

Kühner (2015; based on Hudson and Kühner 2012) utilized fuzzy-set ideal-type analysis (FSITA) to classify the 'protective' and 'productive' welfare properties of 29 countries in Asia and the Pacific. Rooted in the literature on the effects of globalization on contemporary welfare policy, he considered four dimensions of public welfare state activity: two reflecting the key 'protective' dimensions found in employment and social protection programmes, and two reflecting 'productive' dimensions found in education and labour market policy. As such, his analysis examined investment in human resources within and outside of the labour force – key productive elements of welfare consistent with boosting economic output – alongside examination of social protection policies that are designed to ensure income outside of employment or restrict the flexibility of labour markets. With regard to income protection, India is among those countries that have already reached at least lower middle-income status and was judged by the ADB (2013) to have the fiscal space to extend the reach of social protection. For employment protection, the World Bank (2014a) Rigidity of Employment Index, which measures the difficulty of hiring workers, the rigidity of working hours and difficulty/cost of redundancy, suggests that India features comparatively high levels of rigidity – slightly less extensive than Nepal and Pakistan, but stronger than the Maldives, Sri Lanka and Bangladesh. In terms of the general 'ease of doing business', India's global ranking has improved marginally to 130th place in 2015 due to recent reforms making it easier to start a new business and getting electricity (www.doingbusiness.org).

India's investment in education measured as public education spending (for all levels of education) as a share of total public social and education spending (58%) placed it together with Nepal, Bangladesh and the Maldives and relatively further away from Sri Lanka (41%) and Pakistan (85%). As for training, India's large-scale *Mahatma Gandhi National Rural Employment Guarantee Act* (NREGA) has gained much attention in recent years (Fraser 2015). The ADB (2013) suggests that this programme accounted for around 40% of all central government social protection spending in 2009; at the same time, skills development and training investment was almost entirely absent. The formally skilled workforce is in India is estimated to be at a mere 2% (http://labourbureau.nic.in/) and the apparent lack of adequate programmes to train the large number of informal workers has been recognized by the Planning Commission (Government of India 2008, – cited in Batra 2009, p. 350), which stated that this sector:

is not supported by any structural system of acquiring or upgrading skills. By and large, skill formation takes place through informal channels like family occupations, on-the-job training under master craftsmen with no linkage to formal training and certification. Training needs in this sector are highly diverse and multi-skill oriented. Though many efforts for imparting training through a large number of schemes are in place, the outcome is not encouraging.

Based on this empirical analysis, India was classified as a 'weak productive–protective' type featuring relatively strong education investment (in the absence of fiscal commitment to income protection), very low training investment (largely due to the focus on work-for-food programmes) and relatively strong employment protection for a small share of formally employed workers (Kühner 2015, p. 163).

The bifurcated nature of welfare policy in many middle and low-income countries enhances the caution needed when utilizing standard measures of welfare effort at the nation state level. Wood and Gough (2006) emphasize declientalization – that is, the extent to which informal arrangements within the community are characterized by patron-clientelism – in their analysis of welfare regimes in South Asia and redefine the term 'regime' to the most 'general level [as] an institutional matrix of market, state and family forms, which generates welfare outcomes' (Gough 2004, p. 23). Hence, Gough (2004, pp. 33–34) delineates three types of regimes: 'welfare state regimes' in which 'people can reasonably expect to meet (to a varying extent) their security needs via participation in labour markets, financial markets and the finance and provisioning role of a 'welfare state'; 'informal security regimes' in which 'people rely heavily upon community and family relationships to meet their security needs, to greatly varying degrees'; and 'insecurity regimes' in which 'a set of conditions which generate gross insecurity and block the emergence of stable informal mechanisms to mitigate'. According to Gough et al., Asian states are best described as 'informal security' types as minimal social rights, social investment and the productive elements of welfare policy are predominating. Empirical cluster analyses undertaken on a range of welfare input and human development outcome data largely confirm this view: East Asian and Southeast Asian cases are classified as either 'more effective' (Wood and Gough 2006) or 'successful' (Abu-Shark and Gough 2010) informal welfare types; they are thereby clearly and consistently separated from South Asian cases (excluding Sri Lanka), which were labelled as 'less effective-failing informal welfare states' (Ibid.) particularly due to high persisting illiteracy rates among young people.

Kühner's (2015) classification was only based on one point in time (2009–10), while the latest data considered by Gough et al. (Wood and Gough 2006, Abu-Shark and Gough 2010) were from the early 2000s. Even combining the best available quantitative data, together they are therefore unfit for a more dynamic longitudinal consideration of the Indian welfare regime trajectory during the two recent Centre/Left Congress/United Progressive Alliance (UPA) incumbencies (2004–2009; 2009–2014). The question we know turn to is whether India moved beyond its predominantly failing-informal welfare regime features characterized by a weakly developed mix of productive–protective welfare policy interventions, comparatively low social expenditure and mixed social outcomes? It is this question that we know turn to.

3. The Indian welfare regime revisited

The increase in Indian total social protection spending (from 0.4 to 1.5%) between 2005 and 2009 (for which the latest data is available) is impressive (see Table 1).

Table 1. The Indian welfare regime revisited.

Indicator	1990 or earliest	2005 or nearest	2014 or latest	Percentage growth India 2005–2014	Avg. and avg. % growth South Asia[a] 2005–2014
Inputs					
Social protection spending (% of GDP)	–	0.4 (*2004*)	1.5 (*2009*)	275%	2.0 (17%)
Social contributions (% of total revenue)	0.1	0.2	0.2 (*2012*)	0%	1.1 (37%)
Public spending on health (% of GDP)	1.1 (*1995*)	1.0 (*2013*)	1.3 (*2013*)	30%	2.5 (9%)
Private spending on health (% of GDP)	3.0 (*1995*)	3.3	2.7 (*2013*)	−10%	2.5 (0%)
Public spending on education (% of GDP)	2.8 (*1997*)	3.1	3.9 (*2012*)	26%	4.1 (−11%)
Public spending on education (% of total social budget)	–	68.8	58.2	−15%	47.7 (−11%)
Rigidity of employment index (0 = less rigid to 100 = more rigid)	–	–	30	–	26
Outcomes					
GDP per capita (constant 2005 US$)	402.3	729.0	1,235.5	69%	2,041.9 (59%)
Wage and salaried workers (% of total employment)	15.0 (*1994*)	15.6	18.1 (*2010*)	16%	37.2 (..)
Poverty headcount ratio at $3.10 a day (*2011 PPP % of population*)	79.7	73.4	58.0 (*2011*)	−21%	37.8 (−18%)
GINI index of inequality (World Bank Estimate)	30.8	33.4	33.9 (*2010*)	2%	31.4 (−12%)
Secondary female school enrolment (% gross)	34.6 (*1993*)	49.5	69.4 (*2012*)	40%	66.7 (48%)
Youth literacy rate (% of people ages 15–24)	61.9 (*1991*)	81.1	86.1 (*2011*)	6%	77.8 (12%)
Immunization, measles (% of children ages 12–23 months)	56.0	68.0	83.0	22%	89.3 (2%)

Note: Different years due to limited availability of time series data.
Sources: World Bank (2014b), World Development Indicators; Asian Development Bank Social Protection Index. [a]South Asia = Unweighted average for Bangladesh, Bhutan, Maldives, Nepal, Pakistan and Sri Lanka.

Expenditure for labour market programmes, that is, primarily NREGA, increased by 500% from 0.1% of GDP to 0.6% of GDP (ADB 2013). Trends in public health and education spending between 2005 and 2013 have also been positive, namely 30% and 26% increases respectively. While the average public health and education spending is still higher in other South Asian countries (on average), India's higher percentage growth meant that it managed to catch up with its neighbours. Although the share of wage and salaried workers grew by 16% from 2005, formal employment remains only about half the South Asian average (37.2%) and pales in comparison with the shares in Sri Lanka in particular (55.5% in 2010). The relatively slow growth in formal employment in India affected social contributions collected by the Indian government: there has been no increase in social contributions as a share of total revenue in India between 2005 and 2012 according to World Bank data, which is a picture that is very different to other South Asian countries where social contributions in 2012 were on average around five times higher than in India, but also grew at a much faster pace since 2005. Although taxes earmarked for education have increased since 2005 (Palriwala and Neetha 2011), concerns have been raised that the Indian government has focused disproportionately on the expansion of social protection at the cost of other basic public services (Kapur and Nangia 2015).

There have been improvements in both secondary female school enrolment and youth literacy rates in India. This is particularly interesting because – as discussed above – India was classified by Gough et al. among the 'less effective-failing informal welfare states' particularly because of very poor outcomes in youth literacy. The youth literacy rate of India was slightly higher than the South Asian average, but the South Asian percentage growth (12%) was double that of India (6%) from 2005. Indian rates of non-participation in schooling at the pre-school age (6.4%) and the primary school age (12.4%) remain high. Given its large population, India still has the highest total number of children aged between 6 and 13 not in school in South Asia with 11.9 million (UNICEF 2014). High school dropout rates contribute to high inequality in human capital across individual states (Gille 2015), while the available PISA and TIMMS tests suggest that Indian children on the whole perform much worse than their 15-year old peers in neighbouring Southeast Asian countries (Suryadarma and Sumarto 2011). As a consequence, the overall probability of Indian children reaching tertiary education remains very low overall, but particularly so for young girls and students in rural areas (Chakrabarty and Bhaumik 2012). Although improvements in headline figures are clearly visible, India still faces a massive shortage of future skilled labour that stymies productivity.

India's GINI index of inequality stood at 33.9 in 2010, which was a 2% increase of this measure in 2005 according to the World Bank (Table 1). Interestingly, the GINI for the other South Asian countries was not only slightly lower, but also saw a marked decrease over the same period. Solt (2014) computes alternative GINIs on the basis of equivalized household disposable income for India and finds that with a score of 50 in 2005 and 53 in 2010 income inequality in India remained 'extreme' according to the International Labour Organisation's (ILO) classification. At the same time, Solt's (2014) degree of redistribution calculated as the difference between the GINI index at market – that is, before all taxes and transfers – and disposable equivalized household incomes suggests the redistributive effect of Indian welfare policy remained largely negligible. Having said that, India did experience a marked decrease in the poverty headcount ratio at $3.10 a day: a drop from 73.4% in 2005 to 58% in 2012 according to the World Bank. But yet again, this figure remains high in comparison with other South Asian countries. An update of Gough et al.'s cluster analysis with this more recent data suggests that India – together with Bangladesh, Indonesia, the Philippines and Sri Lanka – continues to form a separate welfare regime characterized by relatively low public expenditure on education and healthcare services and mixed outcomes – at best – compared with other South Asian and BRICS countries (see Appendix Table A1).

It does not come as a surprise then that India has been stubbornly placed 135th among 187 countries according to the Human Development Index (UNDP 2014). India also ranked 120th among 128 countries in regard to child malnutrition (International Food Policy Research Institute 2014). Taking a broader perspective, Arora and Ratnasiri

(2015) compute a well-being index consisting of five dimensions, namely knowledge, health, income, technology and infrastructure, and find that not only has the average well-being declined in India for the period 2001–2011 compared with the early 1990s, but also that there has been an escalation of regional disparity across Indian states. Gender inequality in India, in particular, remains epitomized by its ranking of 135th on the United Nations Development Fund's Gender-Related Development Index, a composite index measuring women's status based on female-to-male ratio in per capita income; life expectancy at birth and mean years of schooling (UNDP 2014). Similarly, the Global Gender Gap Index ranks India 101st among 136 countries on the basis of women's economic participation and opportunity, educational attainment, health survival and political empowerment (World Economic Forum 2013). Maybe more worryingly still, the National Sample Survey's (NSS) 66th Employment and Unemployment Survey (EUS) (Government of India 2011) indicated a sharp decline in women's work participation in rural areas by 10.9% between 2005 and 2010; Neff *et al.* (2012) find a contraction of female labour force participation in urban areas from 26.1% to 21.0% too.

Despite an expansion of Indian gross social protection spending effort, we hardly see any immediate impact on the level of statistical redistribution of incomes and no significant shift in the clustering of the Indian welfare regime compared with better performing middle-income countries. India's position on mainstream league tables of human development remains stubbornly low and there is some evidence that overall outcomes even worsened during the 2000s.

4. India's emerging social policy paradigm

Purely quantitative approaches to explore social policy trajectories are often limited especially if they rely on social expenditure figures. As for an analysis of outcomes, there are often substantial time lags before improvements in human development percolate through to the macro level. Capturing underlying changes in social rights are therefore key to better understand the emerging social policy paradigm in India. Figure 1 classifies the key social programmes that were introduced during the two Congress/UPA incumbencies (2004–2009; 2009–2014) along a two-dimensional continuum distinguishing more 'protective' from more 'productive' policies. Although, as a first step, we merely offer a loosely connected list of social policy innovations, a concerted effort to move towards a more 'protective' centre of gravity of the Indian welfare regime becomes evident.

On the far end of the 'protective' scale, we place the *National Food Security Act (NFSA)*, which passed parliament in 2013. Supplementing the Integrated Child Development Programme (ICDS) and the Targeted Public Distribution System (TPDS), NFSA recognizes the right to food as a legal entitlement by providing subsidized food grains to nearly two-thirds of the Indian population living below the poverty line.

The *Indira Gandhi National Old Age Pension Scheme (NOAPS)* was extended in 2007 and is best regarded separately from other social assistance programmes despite sharing stringent means tests to determine eligibility to cash transfers. Additional widow and disability pensions exist: in regard to the former, eligibility extends to abandoned widows or women who are landless or awaiting pending divorce decisions in court, but also women suffering from domestic violence; in regard to the latter, beneficiaries

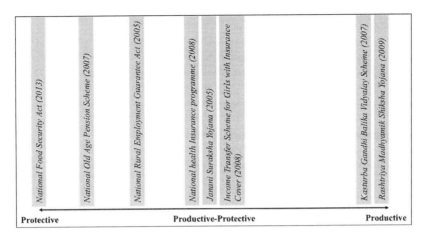

Figure 1. The productive–protective policies of the Indian welfare regime.

should have no source of income, have a disability and be aged 45 or above. Barrientos (2015) points out that social pensions in India have so far not provided a solution to the twin challenges of labour market informality and the low baseline in pension provision.

Also on the 'protective' side of the continuum is the before-mentioned *NREGA*, which was first introduced 2005 and then extended nationally in 2007. NREGA is an anti-poverty programme initiated to provide 100 days of wage employment in the rural areas at the minimum wage level prescribed by the Indian state. In 2011, NREGA provided 2.27 billion days of employment to roughly 53 million households. NREGA employment is seasonal and work is not always available according to workers' demands. There are differences in the implementation of the programme with strong personal or indirect professional links to state parliamentarians and bureaucrats often driving devolved decision-making (Chopra 2011).

The *National Health Insurance Programme* (*Rashtriya's Swasthya Bima Yojana*, RSBY) was launched in 2008 to provide health care to people below the poverty line. It was extended to beneficiaries of NREGA, street vendors, domestic workers and construction workers. At the time of writing, there were 40 million active smart cards and 10 million hospitalization cases according to official Indian government statistics (http://www.rsby.gov.in/). RSBY is means tested and based on poverty line measurements, which some have argued are incongruous with the actual numbers of people at the margins of Indian society; problems of poor usage, lack of quality services and high profit margins of private insurance providers have also been noted (Lagomarsino *et al.* 2012).

Janani Suraksha Yojana (*Protection of Motherhood Scheme, JSY*) is a safe motherhood intervention under the Indian Government's National Rural Health Mission (NHM). It aims to reduce maternal and neonatal mortality by providing financial assistance to pregnant women who give birth after the age of 19 and belong to households below the poverty line (up to two live births). JSY was launched in 2005 and several studies indicate a shift in preferences to hospital-based childbirths since its inception; although principally in line with the WHO's *Global Strategy for Women's and Children's Health* (2010), limited access to transport, poor service quality, high costs in institutions and cultural preferences continue to explain relatively high numbers of home births in India (Ved et al. 2012).

India's cash transfer programmes mainly deal with the issue of discrimination towards young girls in poor households (Barrientos et al. 2010). Given that these programmes are conditional upon criteria such as ensuring immunization or retention in schooling, these programmes mix both 'protective' and 'productive' policy goals and are placed at the 'productive–protective' mid-way point of our classification. The first of these programmes was the *Balika Samridhi Yojana scheme (Girl Child Prosperity Scheme, BSY)*, which started in 1997 and provides post-birth grants for up to two young girls belonging to the same household below the poverty line. The pilot for the *Income Transfer Scheme for Girls with Insurance Cover (Dhanlakshmi, ITSGIC)* started in 2008. Here, income transfers are provided to the family of a female child on fulfilling a set of conditions, that is, birth registration of the child, progress of immunization, enrolment in school.

Several similar state-level programmes exist, but these are not included in Figure 1, mainly for ease of presentation. The *Apni Beti Apna Dhan ('Our daughter, Our Wealth', ABAD)* programme has been operating in Haryana since 1994 and provides a cash transfer to unmarried 18-year-old girls. In 2008, the Delhi government introduced the *Ladli ('Dearest')* scheme to provide households with a second female child with a yearly income transfer for a period of up to 5 years as long as both girls survive. The money is thereby invested in a government fixed deposit and released only when the younger sister turns 18. Similarly, *Mukhyamantri Balika Cycle Yojana (Chief Minister's Scheme for Provision of Bicycles to the Girl Child)* is a conditional cash transfer of the Bihar state government that awards payments to purchase a bicycle to every student enrolled in a standard IX government high school.

Finally, on the 'productive' end of our continuum, the National Programme for Education of Girls at Elementary-Level *(Sarva Shiksha Abhiyan, SSA)* merged with the *Kasturba Gandhi Balika Vidyalay (Kasturba Gandhi Scheme for Provision of Residential School Facilities to the Vulnerable Girls, KGBV)* scheme in 2007 to provide residential schooling for children from communities who live in geographically isolated areas or for girls who have been rescued from child marriages. *Rashtriya Madhyamik Shiksha Yojana (National Middle School/Secondary School Scheme, RMSY)* was launched in 2009 with the objective to improve the quality of secondary education and to make it more widely available. The scheme initially envisaged attaining an enrolment rate of about 75%, or 40 million children, by the end of 2017.

5. Transformative social protection in India?

The overarching aim of this paper is to explore in more detail India's emerging social policy paradigm during the two Centre/Left Congress/UPA governments (2004–2009, 2009–2014). Despite an expansion of social protection spending, we found little evidence that India has moved beyond its failing-informal welfare regime features characterized by a weakly developed mix of productive–protective welfare policy interventions, comparatively low social expenditure and mixed social outcomes. We have also shown that there has been shift of the centre of gravity in Indian social policy towards a more 'protective' approach as the majority of social policy innovations were focused on providing food security, social pensions and cash transfers to poor Indian households. But were these social policy innovations actually transformative? Did they present a qualitative break from previous approaches to social protection in India?

Koehler (2011, pp. 100–101) outlines a useful framework for testing the transformative character of social policy innovations in the Global South. She argues that social protection policies can be regarded as 'transformative' if they meet one or more of six characteristics. First, social policies should be anchored in government fiscal budgets in order to ensure longevity; second, they should be transparent with clear processes by which citizens can claim their social rights; third, they should signify a move towards universal coverage or at least clearly defined categorical entitlements; fourth, they should entail special targeted measures to ensure that women, children and socially excluded groups are able to claim their rights; fifth, they should be designed to consider the preferences and priorities of participants; and sixth, facilitate the creation of productive assets. The creation of 'productive assets' should be of particular interest in India and South Asia as it directly links to current debates about labour market formalization, the facilitation of gender equality, the enhancement of social cohesion and therefore the promotion of more inclusive economic growth (Bonilla-García and Gruat 2003). In the following, we specifically focus on the social policies characterized as 'protective' or 'productive–protective'.

Table 2 presents a crisp (yes–no) classification to classify each of social protection policies discussed above according to Koehler's criteria as a *heuristic* device. The classification of policies is not straightforward and the chosen approach necessarily simplifies otherwise complicated policy detail. Question marks are added to indicate significant

Table 2. Transformative characteristics of social protection in India (2004–2014).

Policies and Programmes	(i) Anchored in government fiscal budgets	(ii) Transparent approach through which citizens can claim their rights	(iii) Move towards universal coverage or categorical entitlements	(iv) Special measures for women, children, Dalits or socially excluded groups	(v) Designed to consider participants' priorities	(vi) Creating productive assets
National Food Security Act (NFSA, 2013)	Yes	Yes	No	Yes	No	No
National Old Age Pension Scheme – (NOAPS, 2007)	Yes	Yes	No	Yes?	No	No
National Rural Employment Guarantee Act (NREGA, 2005)	Yes	Yes	Yes	No	Yes?	No
National health Insurance programme (RSBY, 2008)	Yes	No	No	No	Yes?	Yes?
Janani Suraksha Yojana (JSY, 2005)	Yes	Yes	No	Yes	No	Yes?
Income Transfer Scheme for Girls with Insurance Cover (ITSGIC, 2008)	Yes	Yes	No	No	No	Yes?

differences between policy formulation/intention and delivery. A few notes on the reasons behind our classifications are provided below:

(i) <u>All new government schemes were anchored in government budgets.</u> This is in part indicative of the increased role of government and civil society in designing these policies, but also due to the conceptual contributions from transnational bodies such as the World Bank, UNDP and UNICEF. Improvements in the efficacy in programme implementation can also be attributed to greater involvement of local federal governments and civil society.

(ii) <u>All new government schemes except RSBY followed a transparent right-based approach.</u> For NREGA, the thrust is on the involvement of the *panchayats*, the local self-governments in the rural and urban areas. The other schemes have largely focused on the digitization of claimant records through unique ID numbers albeit with little attention to improving the overall system of cash transfer disbursal. RSBY is classified as an exception because there has been a lack of consensus on what social rights mean in different local contexts (Unnithan and Heitmeyer 2014).

(iii) <u>With exception of the NREGA, none of the new social programmes presented a move towards universal coverage or categorical entitlements.</u> Instead, they are all means tested, based on tight eligibility criteria and characterized by low benefit generosity thus creating a barrier to increased social security coverage. RSBY's particular failure in extending coverage is attributed to poor enrolment, but also deliberate discrimination against poor households by insurance companies (see e.g. Wu 2012). Our classification of NREGA as a 'universal programme' may be controversial as it gives a right to 100 days paid work *only* to rural households; however, NREGA is self-targeting and therefore qualitatively different to the other strictly means-tested social programmes in Table 2 (Barrientos *et al.* 2010).

(iv) <u>With the *exception of NFSA, no targeted* measures for *Dalits* and socially excluded groups have been included.</u> JSY includes additional payments to rural women and to women living in urban areas who give birth in public institutions. Some transport assistance is available too. Special schemes for widows and disabled people also exist under NOAPS, but claimants have to be destitute, abandoned or landless to qualify for transfer payments. Conditionality stipulations are also extremely rigid under ITSGIC and transfers only available to the girls' families either when they turn 18 or complete secondary education. In particular, there is little scope to address risks that are likely to occur before childbirth (Jain *et al.* 2013).

(v) <u>None of the government schemes have been designed in consideration of participants' priorities.</u> A possible exception could be NREGA, which was extended in response to worsening conditions in rural areas (Dubash and Morgan 2012); however, no choice of employment is given to participants. Similarly, although RSBY is available to be used in private and public hospitals, serious deficits in terms of the healthcare infrastructure and human resources severely restrict actual 'consumer choice' (Joumard and Kumar 2015).

(vi) <u>Whether government schemes have led to improvements in productive asset creation remains doubtful.</u> While RSBY and JSY aim to improve accessibility of the poor to health care, the focus on institutional access with little attention to the quality of care remains an issue. As a consequence, its contribution to the creation of productive assets both in terms of physical infrastructure and human resources remains checkered (Joumard and Kumar 2015). Similarly, ITSGIC is not linked with health insurance or education programmes and therefore struggles to address systemic biases against girls and overcome barriers to female employment. NREGA is certainly 'commodifying' in the sense that it presents a right to *unskilled* work, but at its heart it is an anti-poverty programme with little attention to improving participants' skills. Admittedly, there is some evidence that the MREGA's focus on road construction and water supply infrastructure yielded productive assets for individual households or villages, but these effects are merely indirect (Aggarwal et al. 2012).

In light of the above, we have to conclude that although grand in vision, the two Centre/Left Congress/UPA governments (2004–2009, 2009–2014) have adopted a residual, even minimalist, approach to social protection that cannot be judged as fully transformative.

6. Conclusion

While social programmes have existed since India's independence, earmarked fiscal support is now available and the majority of social protection programmes entail clear transparent rules by which citizens can claim their social rights. Yet, the vast majority of social programmes do not signify a genuine move towards more universal coverage or categorical entitlements. Benefit levels remain generally low and eligibility criteria too rigid to facilitate an extension of social protection coverage. There is little evidence of social protection programmes being designed to consider the participants' priorities and their ability to facilitate productive assets *in practice* is questionable. This latter in particular questions whether Indian social policy innovations are sufficient not only to reduce poverty, ill-health and inequality, but also to foster more inclusive economic growth. Despite the emergence of a myriad of social protection policies during the two Centre/Left Congress/UPC governments (2004–2009, 2009–2014), India's social policies essentially remain residual, even minimalist, in character.

This article largely refrained from addressing the politics of social protection in India, but a few concluding remarks are warranted to put the above discussions into broader context. Indian social policy has increasingly played a role in the creation of regime legitimacy, but the shift towards a rights-based political discourse in India stands in sharp contrast to the limited fiscal space of the Indian national state to allocate resources to extend productive and protective welfare policy (Singh 2015). Under the Indian constitution, it is individual states that carry the primary responsibility for implementing and administering social programmes, which explains the large variation in regard to the delivery, efficiency and outcomes of social programmes. Indeed, around 90% of total health and education expenditures are currently contributed by the states. Recent changes in the tax allocations under the Modi government are likely skew the relationship between the national and state governments even further.

Recent social policy initiatives largely appear in fragments with little inter-linkages with each other or any clearly defined road map linked with economic goals of the country. This lack of an overarching strategy might be attributed to poor conceptual clarity, an inadequate evidence base, lack of institutional capacity – political patronage rather than intrinsic realization of citizenship rights. Chatterjee ([1997] 2010,p. 38, cited in, Ehmke 2011,p. 107), points out '[m]ost of the inhabitants of India are only tenuously and even then ambiguously and contextually, rights bearing citizens in the sense imagined by the constitution'. India's democracy has developed into a patronage democracy where politicians maintain close links with their constituencies and where public services such as education, health, minimum standard of living have been sold-off as 'freebies' by the political parties winning elections rather than treating them as genuine social entitlements (Chandra 2004). Not least, Ehmke (2011,p. 109) has argued 'the heterogeneity of [Indian] political society and its politics have been an obstacle for the formation of a common horizon of solidarity [and] continue to form an impediment to redistributive policies'.

Addressing the key developmental challenges India faces will necessitate further-reaching qualitative changes towards a more encompassing and inclusive social protectivism that will in turn help generate productive assets among the Indian poor. Admittedly, the announcement of many new social protection schemes by the new Modi government may force us to change our assessment of the emerging social policy paradigm in India. For instance, the World Bank's Global Findex (Demirguc-Kunt *et al.* 2015) indicates a considerable improvement in access to formal bank accounts (from 35% in 2013 to 53% in 2014) as a consequence of the *Jan Dhan Yojana (Prime Minister's People Money Scheme)* programme, which was launched in 2014 (but see: Aiyar 2014; Ramakumar 2014). If equally successful, the Modi government's ambitious 'Skill India' and 'Make in India' initiatives, which aim to train 500 million Indians and create 100 million new manufacturing jobs by 2022 may well force us to reconsider the Indian political economy altogether. It remains to be seen whether further extensions of the emerging Indian middle class – currently standing somewhere between 100 and 300 million depending on the exact measure used – together with an ever-increasing presence of civil society organizations will trigger not only more domestic demand for manufacturing products, formal employment and the catering for old and new social risks, but also create a new politics of social policy that will manage to move India more genuinely beyond its current pure dependency mode.

Disclosure statement

No potential conflict of interest was reported by the authors.

References

Abu-Shark, M. and Gough, I., 2010. Global welfare regimes: a cluster analysis. *Global Social Policy*, 10 (1), 27–58. doi:10.1177/1468018109355035

Aggarwal, A., Kumar, A., and Gupta, A., 2012. Evaluation of NREGA wells in Jharkhand. *Economic & Political Weekly*, 47 (35), 24–27.

Aiyar, S., 2014. *Jan Dhan Yojana has all the characteristics of those old loan meals*. Available from: http://articles.economictimes.indiatimes.com/2014-09-03/news/53522854_1_jan-dhan-yojana-financial-inclusion-new-account-holders [Accessed September 3 2014].

Arora, R.U. and Ratnasiri, S., 2015. Economic reforms, growth and well-being: evidence from India. *Journal of Economic Policy Reform*, 18 (1), 16–33. doi:10.1080/17487870.2014.920706

Asian Development Bank, 2008. *Strategy 2020: the long-term strategic framework of the Asian Development Bank, 2008–2020*. Mandaluyong City: ADB.

Asian Development Bank, 2013. *The social protection index*. Mandaluyong City: ADB.

Balakrishnan, R., Steinberg, C., and Syed, M., 2013. *The elusive quest for inclusive growth: growth, poverty, and inequality*. Washington, DC: IMF, IMF Working Paper 13/152. doi:10.5089/9781475531169.001

Barrientos, A., 2015. Is there a role for social pensions in Asia? *Asia & the Pacific Policy Studies*, 2 (1), 8–20. doi:10.1002/app5.63

Barrientos, A. and Hulme, D., 2009. Social protection for the poor and poorest in developing countries: reflections on a quiet revolution. *Oxford Development Studies*, 37 (4), 439–456. doi:10.1080/13600810903305257

Barrientos, A., Maitrot, M., and Niño-Zarazúa, M., 2010. *Social assistance in developing countries database*. Manchester: Chronic Poverty Research Centre.

Batra, S., 2009. Strengthening human capital for knowledge economy needs: an Indian perspective. *Journal of Knowledge Management*, 13 (5), 345–358. doi:10.1108/13673270910988150

Bhagwati, J. and Dongardive, M., 2013. *Why growth matters: how economic growth in India reduced poverty and the lessons for other developing countries*. New York, NY: Public Affairs.

Bonilla-García, A. and Gruat, J.V., 2003. *Social protection: A life cycle continuum investment for social justice, poverty reduction and sustainable development*. Geneva: ILO.

Broadberry, S. and Gupta, B., 2010. The historical roots of India's service-led development: a sectoral analysis of Anglo-Indian productivity differences, 1870–2000. *Explorations in Economic History*, 47 (3), 264–278. doi:10.1016/j.eeh.2009.09.004

Bussolo, M. and Lopez-Calva, L., 2014. *Shared prosperity. Paving the way in Europe and Central Asia*. Washington, DC: WB.

Chakrabarty, M. and Bhaumik, S.K., 2012. Whither human capital? The woeful tale of transition to tertiary education in India. *Applied Economics Letters*, 19 (9), 835–838. doi:10.1080/13504851.2011.607109

Chandra, K., 2004. *Why ethnic parties succeed: patronage and ethnic head counts in India Cambridge studies in comparative politics*. Cambridge: Cambridge University Press.

Chatterjee, P., [1997] 2010. Beyond the nation? Or within? *In*: N. Menon, ed. *Empire and nation: Partha Chatterjee: essential writings 1985–2005*. Ranikhet: Permanent Black.

Chopra, D., 2011. Policy making in India: a dynamic process of statecraft. *Pacific Affairs*, 84 (1), 89–107. doi:10.5509/201184189

Cook, S. and Kabeer, N., eds., 2010. *Social protection as development: Asian perspectives.* New Delhi: Routledge.

Demirguc-Kunt, A., et al., 2015. *The global findex database 2014. Measuring financial inclusion around the world.* Washington, DC: WB, Policy Research Working Paper 7255.

Devereux, S. and Sabates-Wheeler, R., 2004. *Transformative social protection.* Brighton: IDS, IDS Working Paper 232.

Drèze, J. and Sen, A., 2013. *An uncertain glory: India and its contradictions.* Princeton: Princeton University Press.

Dubash, N.K. and Morgan, B., 2012. Understanding the rise of the regulatory state of the South. *Regulation & Governance,* 6 (3), 261–281. doi:10.1111/j.1748-5991.2012.01146.x

Ehmke, E., 2011. Political and civil society in India's welfare trajectory. *IDS Bulletin,* 42 (6), 104–110. doi:10.1111/idsb.2011.42.issue-6

Fraser, N., 2015. Social security through guaranteed employment. *Social Policy & Administration,* 49 (6), 679–694. doi:10.1111/spol.2015.49.issue-6

Gille, V., 2015. Distribution of human capital and income: an empirical study on Indian states. *Journal of Macroeconomics,* 43 (March), 239–256. doi:10.1016/j.jmacro.2014.11.003

Gough, I., 2004. Welfare regimes in development contexts: a global and regional analysis. *In:* I. Gough, et al., eds. *Insecurity and welfare regimes in Asia, Africa and Latin America: social policy in development contexts.* Cambridge: Cambridge University Press.

Government of India, 2011. *Employment and unemployment survey: NSS 66th round: July 2009-June 2010, eight quinquennial survey.* New Delhi: National Sample Survey Office.

Hudson, J. and Kühner, S., 2012. Analyzing the productive and protective dimensions of welfare: looking beyond the OECD. *Social Policy & Administration,* 46 (1), 35–60. doi:10.1111/spol.2012.46.issue-1

International Food Policy Research Institute, 2014. *Global hunger index: the challenge of hidden hunger.* Bonn: International Food Policy Research Institute.

International Labour Organisation, 2011. *Social protection floor for a fair and inclusive globalization.* Geneva: ILO, Report of the Social Protection Floor Advisory Group.

International Labour Organisation, 2014a. *World social protection report 2014/15: building economic recovery, inclusive development and social justice.* Geneva: ILO.

International Labour Organisation, 2014b. *Women and men in the informal economy. A statistical picture.* Geneva: ILO.

Jain, N., Singh, A., and Pathak, P., 2013. Infant and child mortality in India: trends in inequalities across economic groups. Journal of Population Research, 30(4), 347-365. doi:10.1007/s12546-013-9110-4

James, K.S., 2011. India's demographic change: opportunities and challenges. *Science,* 333 (6042), 576–580. doi:10.1126/science.1207969

Jones, G. and Ramchand, D., 2013. Education and human capital development in the giants of Asia. *Asian-Pacific Economic Literature,* 27 (1), 40–61. doi:10.1111/apel.2013.27.issue-1

Joumard, I. and Kumar, A., 2015. *Improving health outcomes and health care in India.* OECD Publishing, OECD Economics Department Working Papers, No. 1184. Paris: OECD.

Kapur, D. and Nangia, P., 2015. Social protection in India: a welfare state sans public goods? *India Review,* 14 (1), 73–90. doi:10.1080/14736489.2015.1001275

Koehler, G., 2011. Transformative social protection: reflections on South Asian policy experiences. *IDS Bulletin,* 42 (6), 96–103. doi:10.1111/idsb.2011.42.issue-6

Köhler, U. and Chopra, D., 2014. *Development and welfare policy in South Asia.* New York: Routledge.

Kühner, S., 2015. Analysing the productive and protective dimensions of welfare in the Asia-Pacific: pathways towards human development and income equality? *Journal of International and Comparative Social Policy,* 31 (2), 151–173.

Lagomarsino, G., et al., 2012. Moving towards universal health coverage: health insurance reforms in nine developing countries in Africa and Asia. *The Lancet,* 380 (9845), 933–943. doi:10.1016/S0140-6736(12)61147-7

Mazumdar, S., 2014. India's economy: Some reflections on its shaky future. *Futures*, 56 (2014), 22–29. doi:10.1016/j.futures.2013.10.005

Neff, D., Sen, K., and Kling, V., 2012. *The puzzling decline in rural women's labour force participation in India: a reexamination*. Hamburg: German Institute of Global and Area Studies, GIGA Working Paper No. 196.

Organisation for Economic Co-operation and Development, 2011. *Divided we stand: why inequality keeps rising*. Paris: OECD.

Ostry, J.D., Berg, A., and Tsangarides, C.G., 2014. *Redistribution, inequality, and growth*. Washington, DC: International Monetary Fund, IMF Staff Discussion Note, SDN/14/02. doi:10.5089/9781484352076.006

Palriwala, R. and Neetha, N., 2011. Stratified familialism: the care regime in India through the lens of childcare. *Development and Change*, 42 (4), 1049–1078. doi:10.1111/dech.2011.42.issue-4

Planning Commission, Government of India, 2008. *Eleventh five year plan 2007-2012, vol. 1 – inclusive growth*. New Delhi: Oxford University Press.

Rada, C. and Von Arnim, R., 2014. India's structural transformation and role in the world economy. *Journal of Policy Modeling*, 36 (1), 1–23. doi:10.1016/j.jpolmod.2013.10.013

Ramakumar, R., 2014. *Mirage of Inclusion*. Available from: http://www.frontline.in/the-nation/mirage-of-inclusion/article6412718.ece [Accessed October 3 2014].

Singh, P., 2015. Subnationalism and social development: a comparative analysis of Indian states. *World Politics*, 67 (3), 506–562. doi:10.1017/S0043887115000131

Solt, F., 2014. *The standardized world income inequality database, version 5.0*. Available from: http://myweb.uiowa.edu/fsolt/swiid/swiid.html [Accessed October 2014].

Storm, S. and Naastepad, C.W.M., 2005. Strategic factors in economic development: East Asian industrialization 1950–2003. *Development and Change*, 36 (6), 1059–1094. doi:10.1111/j.0012-155X.2005.00450.x

Surender, R. and Walker, R., 2013. *Social policy in a developing world*. Cheltenham: Edward Elgar.

Suryadarma, D. and Sumarto, S., 2011. Survey of recent developments. *Bulletin of Indonesian Economic Studies*, 47 (2), 155–181. doi:10.1080/00074918.2011.585945

United Nations Childen's Emegency Fund, 2014. *Global initiative on out-of-school children South Asia Regional Study covering Bangladesh, India, Pakistan and Sri Lanka– all children in School by 2015*. Kathmandu: UNICEF.

United Nations Development Programme, 2014. *Human development report 2014. Sustaining human progress: reducing vulnerabilities and building resilience*. New York, NY: UNDP.

United Nations, 2014. *The millennium development goals report*. New York: UN.

United Nations, 2015. *Transforming our world: the 2030 agenda or sustainable development*. New York: UN.

Unnithan, M. and Heitmeyer, C., 2014. Challenges in 'translating' human rights: perceptions and practices of civil society actors in Western India. *Development and Change*, 45 (6), 1361–1384. doi:10.1111/dech.2014.45.issue-6

Ved, R., et al., 2012. Program evaluation of the Janani Suraksha Yojna. *BMC Proceedings*, 6 (Suppl 5), O15. doi:10.1186/1753-6561-6-S5-O15

Wood, G. and Gough, I., 2006. A comparative welfare regime approach to global social policy. *World Development*, 34 (10), 1696–1712. doi:10.1016/j.worlddev.2006.02.001

World Bank, 2014a. *World development indicators*. Available from: http://data.worldbank.org/datacatalog/world-development-indicators [Accessed July 7 2014].

World Bank, 2014b. *Doing business – measuring business regulations*. Available from: http://www.doingbusiness.org/ [Accessed July 7 2014].

World Economic Forum, 2013. *The global gender gap report*. Geneva: World Economic Forum.

Wu, Q., 2012. *What cause the low enrolment rate and utilization of Rashtriya Swasthya Bima Yojana: a qualitative study in two poor communities in India*. Liverpool: Liverpool School of Tropical Medicine.

Appendix

Table A1. Global welfare regime clusters, 2014 or latest available.

Cluster membership	Public spending on health + education (% GDP)	Immunization, measles (% of children ages 12–23 months)	School enrolment, secondary, female (% gross)	Personal remittances, received (% of GDP)	Aid per capita (% GNI)	Life expectancy at birth, total (years)	Literacy rate, youth total (% of people ages 15–24)	Cluster characteristics
Croatia, Estonia, Lithuania, Argentina, Poland, Colombia, Uruguay, Tunisia, Chile, Mexico, Israel, **Korea, Rep.**, Bolivia, Ukraine, Costa Rica	10.1	92.9	99.7	1.9	0.4	76.3	99.0	Good outcomes, high spending
China, Iran, Kazakhstan, Malaysia, Paraguay, Belarus, **Thailand,** Bulgaria, Ecuador, Turkey, Romania,	7.6	96.6	92.2	1.3	0.3	74.1	98.7	Good outcomes, low spending
El Salvador, Jamaica, Nicaragua, **Moldova**	10.1	94.5	77.7	16.6	2.5	72.4	95.1	High spending, high remittances
Bangladesh, India, Peru, Dominican Republic, **Philippines, Sri Lanka**	4.8	87.6	80.3	6.0	0.4	71.3	94.0	Low spending, mixed outcomes
Benin, Ethiopia, Mali, Senegal, Cote d'Ivoire, Guinea-Bissau, Togo, Cameroon, Zambia, Kenya, **Papua New Guinea, Pakistan**	6.4	72.9	38.5	4.0	6.3	58.9	64.6	Poor outcomes, high aid
Botswana, Burundi, Congo, Rep., Ghana, Morocco, Mozambique, Namibia, Rwanda, South Africa, Tanzania, **Nepal, Tajikistan**	10.2	89.2	55.1	1.3	6.7	58.9	85.6	High spending, high aid, improving outcomes

Unweighted cluster averages; hierarchical cluster analysis using Ward linkage method with squared Euclidian Distance, $n = 61$. Detailed findings available upon request.
Sources: World Bank (2014a).

RESEARCH ARTICLE

Pension reform in Germany since the 1990s: new developments and theoretical implications

Liu Tao

ABSTRACT
This article scrutinizes the pension reform in Germany since the 1990s, from two angles: (1) the establishment of a funded pension – the Riester pension plan; and (2) the development of family oriented and gender-neutral pension policies. It argues that the creation of a funded pension scheme in Germany has transcended the conventional distinction between state and market and has resulted in the emergence of a hybrid form of regulatory welfare state and regulated welfare market. From a gender perspective, the current German pension system has become much more gender neutral, 'feminine' and 'family friendly', fundamentally altering the Bismarckian prototype by balancing the pension rights of both sexes. The final section explores the implications of German pension reform for the current situation in China.

Introduction

Conventionally, the pension system in Germany has followed the prototype of Bismarckian social insurance, which was a pioneering model for old-age insurance worldwide. Since the end of the World War II, the Federal Republic of Germany had adhered to a single-pillar model – the statutory pension insurance scheme, which was based on a pay-as-you-go (PAYG) system. However, since the 1970s, challenged by persistent demographic transition and a shift in the share between contributors to and claimants of public pension funds, German policy makers have adopted a more pragmatic attitude towards existing problems (Kaufmann 1997). Through a series of pension reforms since the 1990s, the German pension system has transformed from a single-pillar model to a multi-pillar model. This paradigm shift has been shaped by core reforms – key to these was the adoption of the 'Riester pension reform' in 2002, aiming at the creation and promotion of a pension market heavily regulated by the state regulatory agency. At the programme level, the German pension system converges with the multi-pillar model embraced by more than 100 countries, but unlike the pension market in the Anglo-Saxon and Anglo-American world, Germany has creatively fostered a state-regulated social welfare market shaped by various hyper-complex and rigorous regulatory measures.

Besides the Riester plan, German pension reforms have additionally been concerned with issues of gender, family and childcare. Welfare state researches have assumed that the basic structure of social policy arrangements are shaped by divergent welfare cultures regarding family, childcare and gender (Esping-Andersen 1990, Sainsbury 1994, Siaroff 1994, Lessenich and Borchert 1998). This article argues that pension reforms in Germany have contributed to the formation of a new welfare culture of feminism, which is overwhelmingly based on honouring the 'silent' (but significant) contributions of women to the German welfare state. With regard to the gender issue, a series of pension reforms have resulted in higher gender equality and a power balance between both sexes.

For the sake of the reconfiguration and readjustment of Chinese pension systems, it is very useful to learn from German pension reforms and re-examine the nexus between the state and the market. Moreover, various German experiences might also help China to reconstruct a gender neutral, family oriented and child friendly pension system, which would improve pension equality between both sexes in China.

Analytical framework

The funded pension as an additional pillar and the reconfiguration of the nexus between state and market

Prior to 1980, in the realm of old-age protection, the prevailing social insurance model hinged on the PAYG system in the post-war period in much of the world. At the end of the 1970s, the military government of Chile undertook an unparalleled neoliberal experiment under the special guidance of the Chicago School. This experiment was heavily underpinned by ideological mania aimed at replacing the public pension insurance system with a completely funded system, further strengthening the national capital market. This neoliberal grand reform first attracted the attention of Chile's bordering countries and then was emulated by countries such as Argentina, Paraguay and Columbia (Mesa-Lago 2002, de Mesa and Mesa-Lago 2006, Hu and Manning 2010).

The ideational and structural readjustment of pension schemes in this new wave of reform quickly received the endorsement of the Word Bank. A report published by the World Bank in 1994 entitled 'Averting the old age crisis: Policies to protect the old and promote growth' (World Bank 1994) symbolized a historical turning point in global pension reform. From the perspective of the constellation of actors, a powerful financial organization based on the Bretton Woods System has had tremendous influence in the area of the old-age protection, and the dominant position of the International Labour Organization (ILO), which had prevailed over international pension discourses, was weakened. From the angle of social semantics, the new discourse of 'economic growth' has been embedded into global pension reform. Moreover, demographic discourse and the 'question of sustainability' of a public pension system have been at the top of the agenda for the World Bank. The World Bank publication (1994) corrected the course of the fundamental liberal reform in Chile by advocating a three-pillar model that combines a tax-financed public pension (pillar 1), a mandatory funded system (pillar 2) and individual private savings (pillar 3). Discourse about the multi-pillar model of old-age pension has enjoyed great popularity within global pension reform. Many studies show that this multi-pillar model has spread to various developing countries and transition economies such as those in Central and Eastern Europe and Latin America, as well as GUS states, partially driven by the vast impact of global organizations and partially driven by national policy learning (Vittas 1997, Mesa-Lago 2002, Brooks 2005, Orenstein 2005, 2008). Even pension reforms in the industrialized world have been partially affected by discourse about the multi-pillar pension model (Rutkowski 2004).

Welfare state arrangements are highly associated with the nexus of state and market. Within a comprehensive social welfare system, public agencies and market mechanisms are different providers delivering welfare products. The pension system in modern society is an intermediate policy area that falls between these two core institutions. The modern pension system can be organized through public pension agencies, just as most nations have achieved prior to the great semantic and structural shift that occurred in the 1990s. Pension systems can also dovetail with the liberal logic and ideological paranoia of market fundamentalism. 'Pension privatization can boost national savings' – such a creed is deeply rooted in neoliberal ideology (Mesa-Lago 2002). Privatization of pension systems may strengthen market mechanisms, which can shift the power balance (or imbalance) between the state and the market. Conventionally, pension reform is driven by the ideological rivalry between state and market. The strengthening of one institution will inevitably weaken the other, and the core idea of the clash of pension ideologies is based on an ideational distinction and 'boundary' between state and market (Gilbert 2004). The distinctive boundary between 'public pension' and a 'pension market' is derived from the Hegelian idea of the distinction between state and civil society developed in the early 19th century, and each has developed its own intrinsic and independent functional logic (Kaufmann 2013). German pension reforms have broken through the myth of a bilateral distinction between state and market, representing an innovative case of the entanglement of the two.

Pension policy as family, childcare and gender policy

Conventionally, the welfare state arrangements are concerning the triangle relationship between state, market and family. In addition to the nexus between state and market, it is worth examining the mediation between state and family pertinent to the pension policy. A pension system will sharpen uneven intra-family income redistribution and strengthen gender inequality if pensions are closely linked to income and thus depend only on the earnings of male breadwinners (Esping-Andersen 1990, Sainsbury 1994, Siaroff 1994). In various 'early bird' countries with old-age insurance schemes, pension systems have been 'masculine' rather than 'feminine'. The entitlements of women to a pension have been systematically weakened because female populations normally embody a patchwork employment profile due to the time invested in child rearing and childcare. Female populations normally have a much shorter and sporadic working career, and their income is generally lower than amongst male populations (Kohli 1985). These structurally uneven factors are mirrored in the intra-family distribution of pension income between male breadwinners and female homeworkers. Such inequalities in pension entitlements within families and between both sexes may cement the gender stratification in a society. Whether pension arrangements make intra-family relationships and gender relationships more or less equal depends on how national pension arrangements are developed and designed. National pension policies are able to enhance the status of women in a society through deliberate investment into children's education and care services. Moreover, a family- and child-oriented pension policy can result in more intra-family democracy and a greater level of gender equality through at least partially recognizing the time invested in homework by women as working time.

Pension reform in Germany since the 1990s

Demographic transition and its impact on discourses of pension reform in Germany

In the 1970s, after a period of growth in the birth rate in the post-war period, the total fertility rate (TFR) in major OECD countries started to decline. Since 1975, the TFR in West Germany has declined to 1.5, a figure far below replacement level. In the 1980s, the TFR in Germany declined to its lowest point – 1.28 (Birg 2001). The sharp decline in the TFR and the drastic increase in the average life expectancy have resulted in demographic ageing that has significantly affected the balance between revenue and expenditure within the German pension system (Kaufmann 2005).

The traditional German statutory pension insurance scheme is based on an assumed 'inter-generational contract', which implies a 'latent' social agreement between two generations: the actual pension demands of the generation of the retirees are financed by the pension contributions of those in the contemporary labour market. When the current contributors enter retirement, their pension demands are financed by the generation who is then in the labour market. This kind of inter-generational contract is based on a PAYG system in which current contributors finance the expenses of current pension recipients (Birg 2001).

A sound PAYG system is closely linked to a rational relationship between contributors and recipients. Drastic demographic transition and ageing in Germany have resulted in variable dependency ratios measured by the share of the population aged 60 and over (the current elderly population) and the population between 20 and 59 years old (the current working population). In 1998 in Germany, the dependency ratio was 38.6, and according to demographic forecasts, this figure will increase to 80 or 96 by 2050, which means roughly one employed person must support one elderly person (Birg 2001). Immigration, emigration and the resulting net migration may affect the dependency ratio in the middle term, but net migration per se cannot reverse the ongoing process of demographic ageing. Since the 1990s, challenged by persistent demographic transition, the problems of ageing and the PAYG-based pension system have been widely questioned by scholars and policy-makers in Germany with regard to its sustainability (Marschallek 2004).

Change in policy instruments and policy ideas

The political scientist Hall has developed a theoretical model to delineate policy change by distinguishing first-, second-, and third-order change (Hall 1993). First-order change refers to the alteration of the setting of the policy tool, and second-order change encompasses change in policy tools. The most relevant for the purposes of this article is third-order change, which presumes that in cases of dissatisfaction with the status quo, the policy goal and the frame to understand policy problems are modified. Third-order change labelled as a paradigm shift is comparatively rare because of the restriction of conventional institutions (path dependence) (Hall 1993). The pension reforms in Germany can also be classified according to different levels of policy change.

In the post-war period, an unrecorded consensus was prevalent in Germany, in which it was thought that the net pension replacement rate of the old-age pension should be maintained at about 70% of the earnings of the insured (Döring 2002). Owing to the demography-related shift of the share between contributors and recipients, this tenet of the German pension system has been undermined. The key question now concerns how the system can keep up with the 70% replacement rate under these new circumstances. Various reform concepts have been elaborated, debated or partially put into practice in Germany since the 1990s. The following are the reforms relating to change in policy instruments and policy goals as well as recommendations for reform:

(1) Pension contributions should be raised incrementally. The increase of pension contributions is a pressing issue that has been widely debated in scientific and political circles since the 1990s (Döring 2002). Most scholars and policy makers have acknowledged that the contribution rate for pensions is already too high. It already surpassed 19% in 1986, and afterwards, it was maintained at a very high level until it exceeded 20% in 1997 and 1998 (20.3% in both years; see Figure 1). It soon became clear that there was less space for further increases in pension contributions when the factor of competitiveness in the national economy under the challenge of globalization was taken into consideration. At the dawn of the

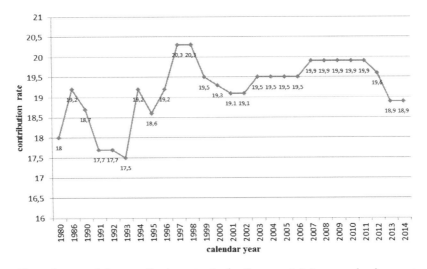

Figure 1. The trajectory of the contribution rates in the German statutory pension insurance scheme between 1980 and 2014. See the development of the contribution rates in the general pension insurance by the Deutsche Rentenversicherung (DRV) at http://www.deutsche-rentenversicherung. de/Allgemein/de/Navigation/6_Wir_ueber_uns/02_Fakten_und_Zahlen/02_kennzahlen_finanzen_ vermoegen/1_kennzahlen_rechengroe%C3%9Fen/entwicklung_beitragssaetze_node.html.

new century, critical voices have emerged that suggest pension contributions should be reduced to a rational level. Some have suggested that German policy makers need to take a bold step to prevent contributions from reaching 22% by 2030 – a critical threshold that will fundamentally jeopardise the status of Germany as an international investment location (Marschallek 2004).

(2) The extension of the retirement age is another issue discussed amongst German politicians and scholars. The basic idea is that every increase in the retirement age will change the ratio between recipients and contributors. But the critical view assumes that the basic question does not relate to the relationship between retirees and employees; rather, it relates to the question of how the labour market can absorb an additional labour force of elderly employees (Schmähl 2009). Moreover, increasing the retirement age is a highly controversial issue that dovetails with diverse interest groups, such as trade unions and industrial associations. Nonetheless, since 2007, there has been incremental reform with a step-by-step increase in the retirement age. According to this reform, the retirement age will be increased from 65 to 67 years from 2012 to 2029, and from 2012 to 2024, it will be increased by 1 month each year. From 2024 to 2029, it will be increased annually by 2 months (see Table 1).

(3) One alternative reform recommendation reaches beyond the pension issue per se. Birg has recommended a population-related concept, suggesting the German government create a more active immigration policy to attract a greater number of young migrants and allow them to enter into the labour market and pay social insurance contributions. The most extreme reform concept proposed by Birg predicts that 188 million foreign immigrants are needed to stabilize the ratio between contributors and recipients in the German social insurance system by

Table 1. Incremental reform through the increase in the retirement age in Germany.

Year of birth	Retirement age for receiving a full pension		Reduced rate when retired at age 65	Calendar year
	Year	Month		
1946	65	0	0.0%	–
1947	65	1	0.3%	2012
1948	65	2	0.6%	2013
1949	65	3	0.9%	2014
1950	65	4	1.2%	2015
1951	65	5	1.5%	2016
1952	65	6	1.8%	2017
1953	65	7	2.1%	2018
1954	65	8	2.4%	2019
1955	65	9	2.7%	2020
1956	65	10	3.0%	2021
1957	65	11	3.3%	2022
1958	66	0	3.6%	2023
1959	66	2	4.2%	2024
1960	66	4	4.8%	2025
1961	66	6	5.4%	2026
1962	66	8	6.0%	2027
1963	66	10	6.6%	2028
1964	67	0	7.2%	2029

Source: German Pension Insurance (Deutsche Rentenversicherung) (2015). See the gradual increase in the retirement age at http://www.deutsche-rentenversicherung.de/Allgemein/de/Navigation/1_Lebenslagen/05_Kurz_vor_und_in_der_Rente/01_Kurz_vor_der_Rente/03_Wann_Sie_in_Rente_gehen_koennen/Wann_Sie_in_Rente_gehen_koennen_node.html.

2050 (Birg 2001). The opponents of this concept warn that not only the quantity but also the quality of immigrants must be taken into consideration. The most pressing concern is how immigrants can be integrated into the host society (Kaufmann 2005).

The migrant crisis in 2015 in Germany, and in particular, the alleged sexual assaults by migrants on New Year's Eve in Cologne, has created an after-shock effect and resulted in politically sensitive debates concerning much more restrictive migration policy. Some right-wing politicians have proposed a temporary closure of the German border with its neighbouring countries. This recent development reveals the complexity of the migration issue. Germany has received over 1 million refugees in 2015, but it is unlikely that these young refugees will mitigate the unfavourable ratio between the number of pensioners and contributors in the German pension system. The central issue remains how successfully these migrants will adapt to German society and how quickly they will be integrated into the German labour market.

Paradigm shift: A German-style funded pension

The Riester pension reform

Beyond the adjustment of pension contributions and the increase in the retirement age, a major pension reform known as the Riester pension reform has fundamentally changed the prototype of the Bismarckian social insurance model.

This reform was pushed through by the ruling parties, the Social Democratic Party (SPD) and the Green Party (Bündnis 90/Die Grünen) in Germany, and was named after the former minister of Labour and Social Affairs – Walter Riester.[1] The original idea was that the replacement rate of the German statutory pension insurance scheme would be reduced from 70% to 67% of the net wage. The reduction in pension would be compensated through an additional funded pension system.

Enacted in 2002, the Riester pension reform is a state-subsidized and privately funded pension provision (Nullmeier 2008). Unlike the prototype of the multi-pillar model proposed by the World Bank (1994), the Riester pension involves a state promoted but voluntary private pension scheme that differs from the pillar of a mandatory funded pension. All employees (other than the self-employed) are entitled to participate in the Riester pension; however, they are not legally obligated to be insured in this funded pension scheme. From the angle of 'compulsory' insurance, the Riester pension scheme significantly differs from the statutory pension insurance scheme.

The prerequisite for participation in the Riester pension requires that insured employees pay 60 € minimum per annum into their Riester accounts. Insured employees in the Riester pension are legally entitled to receive state subsidies if they pay 4% of their average income (before taxes) per annum into their Riester accounts. Contributors can receive a basic allowance (*Grundzulage*) of 154 € per annum, a married couple can receive 308 € per annum, and households with children are in particular promoted by the state through receiving an additional child grant (*Kinderzulage*) in the amount of 300 € per child.[2] If the payments per annum by the contributors are less than 4% of the gross income, the state subsidies are proportionally reduced. The maximum payment into the Riester pension should not exceed 2100 € per annum. Instead of the state subsidies, contributors can alternatively take advantage of a tax preference. All Riester savings up to 2100 € per annum can be claimed as a 'special tax deduction', which means that the Riester savings are exempt from taxes (see Figure 2). However, after retirement, the Riester pension payments are taxable.[3]

Riester clients have to sign a Riester pension contract with one of the financial institutes, bank saving plans, private insurance, private pension funds or fund saving plans in Germany supervised by the state regulatory agency and allowed to manage Riester pension savings. The Riester pension arrangement does not solely reflect the creation of a welfare market driven by neoliberal ideas; this article argues rather that the 'private pension sector' in Germany mirrors a heavily regulated and closely monitored 'pension sector' that is not equivalent to the existing and emerging 'pension market' in Anglo-Saxon countries or in many transition economies. The Riester pension arrangement represents a hyper-complex case of state regulation over the pension market.

The central state regulatory agency is the Federal Financial Supervisory Authority (FFSA).[4] It is fully responsible for the management, monitoring and supervision of the Riester pension investment product. Only if the appropriate actors such as financial institutions have met the minimal regulatory requirements – the so-called certification criteria, then they are allowed to invest the Riester pension savings in the financial market. All Riester pension investment products are certificated by the FFSA.

The requirements set by the FFSA include the following[5]:

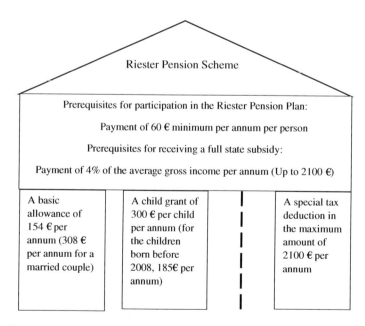

Figure 2. The Riester pension scheme in Germany: a privately funded pension provision promoted by state subsidies or tax preference. Source: Author's compilation. See the webpage of FMJCP at http://www.gesetze-im-internet.de/estg/BJNR010050934.html#BJNR010050934BJNG023502140.

(1) The payment of the Riester pension shall only be allowed to commence after the age of 60. Early payment of the Riester pension is not allowed.
(2) During the pension payment stage, prior pension contributions and the additional state subsidies paid into the Riester pension accounts (as a minimum amount of Riester pensions) shall be guaranteed.
(3) The Riester pension contracts shall be fully gender neutral.[6]
(4) Financial institutes will ensure a lifelong pension payment for Riester clients.
(5) Riester investors will be regularly informed by financial providers about the investment portfolio, the structure of the investment funds and the possible risks of the investment.
(6) The Riester pension contracts and the capital contained within it cannot be pledged, and they are not subject to insolvency.

Only when the above-mentioned requirements have been met can an investment product be certified. These comprehensive supervisory measures of the FFSA must conform to the Retirement Assets Act (*Altersvermögensgesetz*) enacted in 2002 by the German federal parliament. The central target of the German pension supervisory regime is to ensure the transparency of the pension market and avoid the mismanagement or gambling and misuse of pension funds.

As Figure 3 shows, the operation of the Riester pension involves multiple stakeholders. Individual policyholders – Riester investors – must sign a Riester contract with a certified financial institute into which they pay pension contributions. After retirement, the institute pays out the pension and interest to policyholders according to the terms of the contract. The Riester pension participants apply for state subsidies from the Central Benefit Agency, which will deposit these subsidies into the Riester accounts. If the policyholders prefer a model of tax preference and deduction, they can apply for a tax refund from the tax office.

The Riester pension reform and the partial privatization of the German pension system have triggered debates over the problems derived from this paradigmatic transition. The Riester pension may have a marginal effect on low-income individuals and families as well as on households without any regular income since they do not have the necessary financial resources to pay the extra Riester contributions. Consequently, the Riester pension may favour the middle or upper-middle classes. The question of 'pension justice' has thus arisen (Schmähl 2009), since those who engage in

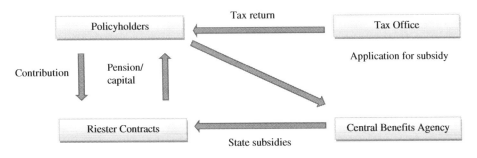

Figure 3. Operation of the Riester pension. Source: Author's compilation.

atypical and irregular employment in the labour market are actually excluded from the Riester pension. Old-age poverty is preprogramed and many retired people in Germany are increasingly exposed to risk of poverty in their old age (Hinrichs 2008).

Theoretical implications of the Riester pension reform

Statutory old-age insurance (pillar 1), the previously existing but now extended company pension scheme (pillar 2) and the Riester pension (pillar 3) together constitute the German-style multi-pillar insurance scheme. The third pillar of the German pension system – the Riester pension – resembles the second pillar in the multi-pillar model proposed by the World Bank (1994). However, the German-funded pension system differs considerably from the World Bank's second pillar and the funded-pension systems in various transition economies.

First, the second pillar endorsed by the World Bank is a mandatory pillar rather than a voluntary option; in contrast, the German third pillar lacks the coerciveness of law. It is based on the free participation of German employees. Similarly, the German third pillar differs from its own first pillar – mandatory public insurance. Second, according to the World Bank's policy recommendation, the second pillar – a mandatory funded pension – plays a decisive role in the overall pension system, and in the practices of various transition countries, the mandatory funded pension is proportionally as important as the public pension if not more so. In Germany, the significance of the public pension is still much higher than the funded pension. Compared with statutory pension insurance, which still embodies the institutional purpose of maintaining a replacement level of 67%, the Riester pension plays only a marginal role in the overall pension system. Third, unlike the ultimate goal of the World Bank and of many transition economies in Central and Eastern Europe, Latin America and Commonwealth of Independent States seeking incremental substitution of the PAYG system through a mandatory funded system, the German pension system does not seek a fundamental reversal of its pension system. The third pillar fulfils instead a supplementary function to the prevailing pillar – the public pension (see Table 2).

The most intriguing sociological observation of German pension reform concerns the blurring of boundaries between state and market. Unlike the drastic market-oriented pension reforms in new emerging markets, and unlike the welfare market sector in the Anglo-Saxon and Anglo-American world, the German pension market is a heavily regulated welfare sector. Comprehensive and rigorous public laws, strongly shaped by

Table 2. Comparison of the funded pension in the German and World Bank multi-pillar insurance models.

	German multi-pillar model	World Bank multi-pillar model
Coerciveness of the funded system	Non-obligatory	Mandatory
Role of the funded system in the overall pension system	Marginal	Central
Relation of the funded system to the public pension	Supplementary	Substitutive
Ultimate target of reform	Maintaining the supremacy of the public pension system	Substitution of the PAYG-system through a funded system

Source: Author's compilation.

the tradition of state regulation over the market prevalent in the German model of a 'social market economy', have set the line of demarcation for safe and responsible investment. This structure has profoundly shaped an intermediary sphere that links market mechanisms to a public policy field. Rigorous administration and heavy regulation through the welfare state has resulted in an emergent hybrid welfare sector, which engages multiple stakeholders: a supervisory agency, consumer protection agencies and financial actors. This new form of hybridized sector has been labelled a 'regulatory welfare state', social policy regulation or a 'welfare market' by German scholars (Nullmeier 2001, 2008, Berner 2004, 2007, 2008, Leisering 2008) signifying a fundamental semantic and structural transition from the conventional welfare state. The transition from a providential welfare state to a regulatory welfare state mirrors a fundamental reconfiguration of the nexus between state and market rather than a simple social-technological type of reform.

The basic rhetoric of reform is as follows: market forces have on the one side been applied to tackle pension problems that cannot completely be resolved through a sole public pension system, and on the other side, the 'destructive forces' of the financial market should be rigorously constrained and regulated by the state.

Leisering has highlighted the most significant trends in the Riester pension reform. The first concerns the internationalization of values; the investment and return of the Riester pension funds are closely linked to European and global financial markets. The public pension pillar in the traditional sense is regulated by national policy; in contrast, the policy domain of the Riester pension scheme dovetails with economic and financial globalization (Leisering 2008). The second trend is associated with the reinvigoration of civil laws in the area of social protection. Historically, the development and extension of public policy has been a process of the decoupling of social and public laws from civil laws. In other words, public laws have become an independent legal area, differing significantly from civil laws. However, the establishment of the Riester pension has resulted in rigorous state intervention in capital and consumer markets. One of the central tasks of welfare state regulation is to protect the consumer's rights, which are framed and regulated by civil laws. In this case, civil laws are 'returned' to the traditional domain of public policy regulated by public laws (Leisering 2008). The third trend reflects the fact that state regulatory methods over a regulated pension market have become hyper-complex, because the investment methods and risks involved have tremendously increased in a globalized financial market. The state is relying on more precise socio-technological methods and hyper-complex statistical models to tackle the possible problems associated with the speculation of pension funds in the pension market. Grand ideologies about social welfare have been gradually substituted by socio-technocratic governance (Leisering 2008).

Pension reforms and their impact on issues of family, childcare and gender

Welfare state arrangements might fulfil the function of narrowing the structural inequality between social classes or between sexes; however, a stratified social welfare system can also result in perpetuating or even widening social inequality (Esping-Andersen 1990, Sun and Liu 2014). Pension system arrangements also operate like a double-edged sword regarding the narrowing and diminishing of social inequality and injustice. They can on the one hand help to reduce social and economic disparities. On the other hand, they can cement existing social stratification. Whether the pension system fulfils an equalizing function or the function of preserving social stratification depends on how the pension arrangements have been designed and structured.

The traditional German model of a Bismarckian old-age insurance system is designed to preserve intra-family power distribution. Entitlement to a 'dignified' pension was based on a male breadwinner model closely related to an uninterrupted and gapless employment biography of husbands in the labour market (Kohli 1985, Döring 2002). The status of wives was rather dependent and subordinate. Husbands were responsible for the family's expenses and they would ostensibly provide pension income for the entire family after they retired. The traditional German statutory old-age pension insurance was thus a highly 'masculine' gender-divided system that assumed a wife's dependency on her husband. After the husband passed away, the wife was able to receive a widow's pension.

However, since the late 1980s, a series of pension reform policies related to the issue of gender have transformed the prototype of the conventional Bismarckian pension system, reshaping intra-family and gender relationships significantly. The German pension system has evolved into a more a family oriented, 'feminine' and 'gender-equal' system.

The pension reform in 1986 provided women with children 'contribution-free child-care years', in which 2 years of child-care were counted as qualifying periods towards pension entitlement. In 1992, with the enactment of a new pension reform law, the contribution-free child-care period was extended to 3 years. These pension reforms contributed to recognition of women's contributions to the German social welfare state and the safeguarding of women's pension rights (Bäcker et al. 2010).

Traditionally, in the German pension system, non-working wives were fully dependent on their husbands' incomes. After husbands passed away, a widow's pension was granted. Currently, the concept of 'pension splitting' (*Rentensplitting*) provides an alternative model of gender-neutral pension payment. Couples in Germany can now choose to split their pension entitlements into two parts. This gender-based model provides for pension rights to be distributed equally, and in this case, the widow's pension has been dropped (Bäcker et al. 2010). The concept of pension splitting favours in particular wives with no source of income, marginal income or a discontinuous employment biography, who are thus located in a disadvantaged position with regard to receipt of a pension.

In the Riester pension scheme, issues of child rearing and gender equality have also been taken into account. Households with children are recompensed by the Riester pension system through receiving special child grants per annum (see the previous section). As a private pension product, the Riester pension had initially accounted for the differential risks based on sex. Since the average life expectancy of a woman is longer and her average income is lower than that of a man, female Riester investors had to pay 15% more in contributions to achieve the same pension benefits as male investors. However, in 2006, a unisex tariff was adopted by the German federal parliament, enforcing a ban on gender-related discrimination. Since then, women and men have enjoyed a fully equal pension based on their contributions (Kopischke and Leisering 2007, Leisering and Vitic 2009).

Through a series of reforms, the German pension system has reduced gender-related disparities, and the stratification of both sexes has been flattened significantly. Moreover, through dovetailing with family policy and child policy, pension systems are deeply implicated in the promotion of families and childcare. From a long-term perspective, the German old-age pension system might have an impact on the rise of the birth rate.

The implication of the German pension reforms for china

Over the last two decades, Germany has abandoned its single-pillar paradigm and adjusted itself to a multi-pillar insurance model, conforming to the pension reforms in most countries in the world. The central reform policy in Germany has been to create a voluntarily funded pension pillar subsidized by the state and to promote a welfare market heavily regulated by the state regulatory agency. A regulatory welfare state and a regulated welfare market have replaced the conventional model of a providential welfare state. This innovative reform may favour and encourage idea transfer and policy learning between China and Germany. Conventionally, pension reforms and the adjustment of the weight of different pension pillars in China have been ideologically tainted. Various grand ideologies such as statism and neoliberalism periodically pull pension reform in different directions. If a public pension has been given more weight in a particular cycle of reform, this reform has been to a certain degree paraphrased as a 'victory' for the state.[7] On the contrary, if a funded pension has been given more weight, such reform could be easily interpreted as the supremacy of market fundamentalism. Chinese pension reforms have periodically oscillated between rival ideologies and target conflicts (Leisering *et al.* 2002, Liu 2005, Shi 2006, Liu and Sun 2015).

The German style of funded pension has provided an alternative model, transcending the classic notions of state and market derived from Hegelian philosophy and showing that the institutional boundaries between the two are being gradually blurred. Public and private institutions are increasingly being combined and synthesized. The 'visible foot' of the state has stepped on the 'invisible hand' of the market by rigorously regulating, controlling and supervising market access, investment methods, investment portfolios and risk calculation in the pension market. In this case, the classic 'market' is no longer a market, and the classic welfare state is no longer a providential or a care state. Their roles, targets and responsibilities have shifted through the mutual entanglement of state and market actors, and a hybrid sector mediating between state and private actors has emerged. The reconfiguration of the relationship between state and market might provide useful ideas for Chinese pension reforms, which are still profoundly shaped by the classic notion of a distinction between state and market.

Some pension reforms in Germany are concerned with issues of family, children and gender. As various welfare state theorists have proposed, welfare state arrangements may not necessarily narrow the gap between social classes; they can also lead to the cementing and preservation of social stratification (Esping-Andersen 1990). A 'masculine' pension system can have a strong negative effect on intra-family power balance and gender equality, and it might also play a counterproductive role in the development of birth rates. The traditional German statutory pension insurance system was strongly oriented towards a 'man-centred' system that mitigated the self-initiative and independence of women and prevented them from being emancipated from a gender stratified pension system. However, via a series of reforms over the last two decades, the German pension system has become increasingly gender neutral, 'feminine' and family oriented. Counting the child-rearing period as a compulsory contribution period, pension splitting between husbands and wives, granting child allowances and the adoption of a unisex tariff in the Riester pension plan have all contributed to this transformation. These reforms have significantly altered the prototype of the Bismarckian social insurance model, making the modern version of the German pension system much more gender equal.

Compared with the gender-neutral pension policy in Germany, gender issues and the promotion of families and children are completely neglected within Chinese pension policy. Thus, German experiences deserve more attention from Chinese scholars and policy makers. Currently, China is facing the dawning of a new era: the TFR in China is far below the replacement level, which will hinder long-term social and economic development tremendously. Even the relaxation of the one-child Policy cannot reverse the extremely low desire for children amongst many young Chinese couples. It is exactly the time to consider introducing a more gender equal and family-oriented pension policy to protect women's pension rights and stimulate birth rates.

Is the German model of a pension system and pension reform learnable and replicable for China? Some historic and institutional legacies suggest that a policy transfer between Germany and China is possible. Welfare state researchers have noted that Northeast Asian countries such as China, Japan and South Korea have adopted mostly the Bismarck type of social security, which means that a social insurance scheme financed by contributions is predominant in this region. Learning from social policy reforms of Germany is indeed prevalent in Northeast Asian countries. For instance, China has partially copied the German model of statutory accident insurance since 2004 (Leisering and Liu 2010, Liu 2015), and South Korea and Japan have emulated the long-term care insurance scheme in Germany and have created their own care insurance arrangements via learning and borrowing German ideas (Leisering 2005). This institutional affinity and the cognitive learning tradition between Northeast Asia and Germany may encourage idea transfer from Germany to China. The major factor hampering policy learning is that China remains a 'backward' gender welfare regime (Liu and Sun 2015). The awareness of a gender-related problem has not taken shape yet, and the idea of a gender-neutral and gender-equal pension has not reached the social and political agenda until most recently, remaining thus a peripheral issue in the national pension debates in China.

Notes

1. The Riester Pension Reform was promoted by the government of Schröder (SPD) and Fischer (Alliance '90/Green) in the legislative period between 1998 and 2005. Although the SPD and the Green Party pursue the target of social democracy and social and ecological justice, this red-green coalition has promoted surprisingly the most liberal and most controversial reforms in the history of the German welfare state, including the adoption of the Riester pension, the tremendous transition of labour market policy and the unemployment insurance system through reduction of social welfare benefits (the so-called Hartz IV reform) and liberal reform of the health insurance system.

2. If the children were born before 1 January 2008, the child grants amount to 185 €.
3. Data source: Federal Ministry of Justice of Consumer Protection, http://www.gesetze-im-internet.de/estg/BJNR010050934.html#BJNR010050934BJNG023502140.
4. In German it is called *Bundesanstalt für Finanzdienstleistungsaufsicht* (Abbreviation: *BaFin*).
5. On the requirements for the certification of the Riester pension products, see the webpage 'old age pension provision – Riester pension plan', http://www.altersvorsorge-riester-rente.net/.
6. This gender-related policy will be exemplified in the Section "Pension reforms and their impact on issues of family, childcare and gender".
7. Inspired by the proposal of a multi-pillar pension system by the World Bank (1994) the Chinese government has installed a two-pillar pension scheme for the urban employees since 1997: the first pillar is an earning based pension based on the PAYG principle, with a defined-benefit portion; the second pillar is a capital funded and defined-contribution pension relied on mandatory private savings. These two pension pillars cover the urban employees in the formal sector and they are employment related and co-financed by the contributions of employers and employees. The first pillar is included to the array of the public policy issues, the second pillar is however more associated with the market mechanisms. The debates on the pension reforms in China are marked by ideologically tinged rhetoric and remain highly contested, since left-wing scholars usually advocate strengthening the first pension pillar, and the liberal scholars prefer to adopt the second pillar to boost the capital market and increase the national capital accumulation in China (Liu 2005, Liu and Sun 2016). Recently, the Chinese government has adopted a non-contributory basic pension (*jichu yanglaojin*) in order to cover the rural residents and the urban non-employed workers. This basic pension actually constitutes the zero pillar of the Chinese pension arrangement (Liu and Flöthmann 2013).

Disclosure statement

No potential conflict of interest was reported by the author.

References

Bäcker, G., et al., 2010. *Sozialpolitik und soziale Lage in Deutschland. Band II*. Wiesbaden: Verlag für Sozialwissenschaften.
Berner, F., 2004. Wohlfahrtsmarkt und wohlfahrtsstaatliches Arrangement. Marktstrukturen und sozialstaatliche Einbettung der kapitalgedeckten Altersvorsorge in Deutschland. REGINA-Arbeitspapier Nr. 6. Bielefeld: University Bielefeld.
Berner, F., 2007. *Der entgrenzte Sozialstaat. Der Wandel der Alterssicherung in Deutschland und die Entzauberung sozialpolitischer Fiktionen*. Doctoral thesis. University Bielefeld.
Berner, F., 2008. *Der hybride Sozialstaat. Die Neuordnung von öffentlich und privat in der sozialen Sicherung*. Frankfurt: Campus Verlag.
Birg, H., 2001. *Die demographische Zeitenwende. Der Bevölkerungsrückgang in Deutschland und Europa*. München: Verlag C.H. Beck.

Brooks, S.M., 2005. Interdependent and domestic foundations of policy change: the diffusion of pension privatization around the world. *International Studies Quarterly*, 49 (2), 273–294. doi:10.1111/isqu.2005.49.issue-2

de Mesa, A.A. and Mesa-Lago, C., 2006. The structural pension reform in Chile: effects, comparisons with other Latin American reforms, and lessons. *Oxford Review of Economic Policy*, 22 (1), 149–167. doi:10.1093/oxrep/grj010

Döring, D., 2002. *Die Zukunft der Alterssicherung. Europäische Strategien und der deutsche Weg*. Frankfurt am Main: Suhrkamp.

Esping-Andersen, G., 1990. *The three worlds of welfare capitalism*. Cambridge: Polity Press.

Gilbert, N., 2004. *Transformation of the welfare state: the silent surrender of public responsibility*. Oxford: Oxford University Press.

Hall, P.A., 1993. Policy paradigms, social learning, and the state: the case of economic policy making in Britain. *Comparative Politics*, 25 (3), 275–296. doi:10.2307/422246

Hinrichs, K., 2008. Kehrt die Altersarmut zurück? Atypische Beschäftigung als Problem der Rentenpolitik. *In*: G. Bonoli and F. Bertozzi, eds. *Neue Herausforderungen für den Sozialstaat*. Bern: Haupt Verlag, 19–37.

Hu, A.Q. and Manning, P., 2010. The global social insurance movement since the 1880s. *Journal of Global History*, 5 (1), 125–148. doi:10.1017/S1740022809990350

Kaufmann, F.X., 1997. *Herausforderungen des Sozialstaates*. Frankfurt am Main: Suhrkamp.

Kaufmann, F.X., 2005. *Schrumpfende Gesellschaft: vom Bevölkerungsrückgang und seinen Folgen*. Frankfurt am Main: Suhrkamp.

Kaufmann, F.X., 2013. *Variations of the welfare states: Great Britain, Sweden, France and Germany between capitalism and socialism*. Berlin: Springer.

Kopischke, I. and Leisering, L., 2007. Grenzen marktregulativer Politik – Die europäische Debatte zu "Unisex-Tarifen" in der privaten Altersvorsorge. Regina – Arbeitspapier Nr. 25. Bielefeld: Bielefeld University

Kohli, M., 1985. Die Institutionalisierung des Lebenslaufs. Historische Befunde und theoretische Argumente. *Kölner Zeitschrift Für Soziologie Und Sozialpsychologie*, 37 (1), 1–29.

Leisering, L., Gong, S., and Hussain, A., 2002. *People's Republic of China – old-age pensions for the rural areas: from land reform to globalization*. Manila: Asian Development Bank.

Leisering, L., 2005. Social policy learning und Wissensdiffusion in einer globalisierten Welt. *In*: U. Becker, G.C. Zheng, and B. Darimont, eds. *Grundfragen und Organisation der Sozialversicherung in Deutschland und China*. Baden-Baden: Nomos, 73–95.

Leisering, L., 2008. Soziale Regulierung privater Altersvorsorge in Deutschland. Instrumente, Normen und ordnungspolitische Herausforderungen. DRV-Schriften Band 80, Alterssicherung im Mehr-Säulen-System: Akteure, Risiken, Regulierungen. Jahrestagung 2008 des Forschungsnetzwerks Alterssicherung (FNA) am 24. und 25. Januar 2008 in Berlin.

Leisering, L. and Vitic, I., 2009. Die Evolution marktregulativer Politik. Normbildung in hybriden Bereichen sozialer Sicherung – das Bespiel der Uni-Sex Tarife für die Riester-Rente. *Zeitschrift Für Sozialreform*, 55 (2), 97–123.

Leisering, L. and Liu, T., 2010. Globale Wissensdiffusion in der Sozialpolitik. Die Einführung einer Arbeitsunfallversicherung in der Volksrepublik China. *Zeitschrift Für Sozialreform*, 56 (2), 175–206.

Lessenich, S. and Borchert, J., 1998. *Welten des Wohlfahrtskapitalismus: der Sozialstaat in vergleichender Perspektive*. Frankfurt am Main: Campus Verlag.

Liu, T., 2005. Die Reform der Alterssicherung in der VR China: Entwicklung und Determinanten. Master thesis. Bielefeld University.

Liu, T. and Flöthmann, E.-J., 2013. The new aging society: demographic transition and its effects on old-age insurance and care of the elderly in China. *Zeitschrift Für Gerontologie Und Geriatrie*, 46 (5), 465–475. doi:10.1007/s00391-012-0401-8

Liu, T., 2015. *Globale Wissensdiffusion in der Politik sozialer Sicherung: Die Einführung einer gesetzlichen Unfallversicherung in der Volksrepublik China*. Frankfurt am Main: Lang.

Liu, T. and Sun, L., 2015. Maternity insurance in China: global standards and local responses. *Asian Women*, 31 (4), 23–51. doi:10.14431/aw.2015.12.31.4.23

Liu, T. and Sun, L., 2016. Pension reform in China. *Journal of Aging & Social Policy*, 28 (1), 15–28. doi:10.1080/08959420.2016.1111725

Marschallek, C., 2004. Die "schlichte Notwendigkeit" privater Altersvorsorge. Zur Wissenssoziologie der deutschen Rentenpolitik. *Zeitschrift Für Soziologie*, 33 (4), 285–302.

Mesa-Lago, C., 2002. Myth and reality of pension reform: the Latin American evidence. *World Development*, 30 (8), 1309–1321. doi:10.1016/S0305-750X(02)00048-7

Nullmeier, F., 2001. Sozialpolitik als marktregulative Politik. *Zeitschrift Für Sozialreform*, 47 (6), 645–668.

Nullmeier, F., 2008. Der Aufstieg der Wohlfahrtsbranche. Folgerungen für die Sozialpolitikforschung. DRV-Schriften Band 80, Alterssicherung im Mehr-Säulen-System: Akteure, Risiken, Regulierungen. Jahrestagung 2008 des Forschungsnetzwerks Alterssicherung (FNA) am 24. und 25. Januar 2008 in Berlin.

Orenstein, M.A., 2005. The new pension reform as global policy. *Global Social Policy*, 5 (2), 175–202. doi:10.1177/1468018105053678

Orenstein, M.A., 2008. *Privatizing pensions: the transnational campaign for social security reform*. Princeton: Princeton University Press.

Rutkowski, M., 2004. Home-made pension reforms in Central and Eastern Europe and the evolution of the World Bank approach to modern pension systems. *In*: M. Rein and W. Schmähl, eds. *Rethinking the welfare state. The political economy of pension reform*. Cheltenham: Edwards Elgar Publishing, 319–334.

Sainsbury, D., 1994. *Gendering welfare state*. London: Sage Publication.

Schmähl, W., 2009. *Soziale Sicherung. Ökonomische Analysen*. Wiesbaden: Verlag für Sozialwissenschaften.

Shi, S.-J., 2006. Left to market and family – again? Ideas and the development of the rural pension policy in China. *Social Policy & Administration*, 40 (7), 791–806. doi:10.1111/spol.2006.40.issue-7

Siaroff, A., 1994. Work, welfare and gender equality: a new typology. *In*: D. Sainsbury, eds. *Gendering welfare state*. London: Sage Publication, 82–100.

Sun, L. and Liu, T., 2014. Injured but not entitled to legal insurance compensation – ornamental institutions and migrant workers' informal channels in China. *Social Policy & Administration*, 48 (7), 905–922. doi:10.1111/spol.2014.48.issue-7

Vittas, D., 1997. The Argentine pension reform and its relevance for Eastern Europe. Policy research working paper of the World Bank. Washington: World Bank Group.

World Bank, 1994. *Averting the old age crisis: Policies to protect the old and promote growth*. Washington: World Bank.

RESEARCH ARTICLE

Social decentralization: exploring the competitive solidarity of regional social protection in China

Shih-Jiunn Shi

ABSTRACT
This article elaborates on the theoretical issues related to the decentralization of social provision within China's reform contexts. The major contention is that, due to the specific Chinese style of central–local relations, social decentralization has set in motion a set of complex interactions between central and local governments, and among the regions with regard to economic competition and social integration. Three different but interrelated modes of territorial politics in social protection are discussed. These are (1) social dumping, in which regions compete to attract inward investments or subsidies from above at the expense of distributional objectives; (2) regional protectionism, in which well-off localities tend to erect administrative barriers to prevent "welfare migration" from other regions; and (3) intricate central coordination of local implementation that renders social policy development even more regionalized, with only the least common denominator (i.e. minimum benefit levels set in major social programmes) applicable across the country while supplementary benefits remain variegated across the regions. In all three cases, regional inequality and interregional redistribution have risen to significance in Chinese social politics as enormous regional variation in the provision of public goods and services persists. These developments of social decentralization have important implications for understanding the social governance and future direction of social policy in China.

Introduction

China's social security systems have undergone great transformations since the reforms in 1979. In the transition to a market economy, the state has overhauled the existing socialist welfare institutions and shifted welfare responsibilities from the urban workplace and rural commune to the civil society and individuals. Especially since the 2000s, institution-building and institution-consolidation have gained momentum in almost all social security domains, as outlined in the recent approach of "urban–rural harmonization" that aims to obliterate the urban–rural divide in social citizenship (Saich 2008, Zhao and Lim 2010). A noteworthy phenomenon has been successive fiscal and administrative reforms that have expanded the role of local government from service provision to benefit finance. Especially the provinces or prefectures are expected to shoulder the financial burden (pooling) of social insurance and social assistance. This is even more the case in rural social security, most programmes of which are organized at the village level, whereas their operation and financing also rest with lower tier governments (prefecture at best; see Hussain 2007). Central government often plays the role of policy coordination and supervision, defining the broad national policy frameworks and principles without specific details of how they should be transposed.

One result of the decentralized delivery of public resources is the growing variation of subnational social policy. Partly out of the Maoist legacy that each locale should get along with its own resources, and partly due to the gradualist approach, the central government relies on its subordinate government tiers to grope for appropriate social policies in accord with local circumstances. Formal institutionalization through central statutory promulgation often comes at a much later stage following successive local policy experimentation. Various social policy domains demonstrate differentiated institutional dynamics and regional variety.

The scholarship of Chinese politics has concentrated on the changing nature of central–local relationship in the reform era (for an overview, see Zheng 2007, Li 2010). In economic and fiscal policies alike, numerous research findings identify the role of local governments in spurring local developments that have amounted to rapid economic growth at the national level for decades (e.g. Walder 1995, Oi 1999, Whiting 2001). Motivations behind the economic robustness were often linked with the potential prospect of personal career of local cadres in case of strong local economies, and the profuse local revenues that enabled further economic investment or infrastructure improvement. Indeed, throughout the 1980s and 1990s, the central government has successfully stimulated the interests of its subordinate officials in the "GDP-ism", with the evaluation of the leadership management system that overwhelmingly lays emphasis on economic performances. Furthermore, local governments have enjoyed considerable discretionary powers in terms of fiscal and economic policymaking and implementation, which laid the institutional foundation for the pursuit of local growth (Montinola et al. 1995, Huang 1996, Cao et al. 1999).

Within China's authoritarian political system, decentralization is certainly not a one-way route as the central government still wields crucial control mechanisms to curtail the scale of local deviation. Some studies even lend greater importance to the central control, maintaining that local autonomy only reaches so far as the central government circumscribes (Cai and Treisman 2006). By the same token, an emerging direction is also discernible, coined in the term "soft centralization" that characterizes recent efforts of the central government to concentrate the powers to the upper administration level (mostly province and prefecture), leaving its lower echelons such as the township governments to become "hollow shells" (Mertha 2005, Smith 2010). According to this argumentation, decentralization is at best political experimentation of the party state in its adaptation to the changing economic circumstances while not losing its grip on the local governments. "Competition under hierarchy" or "experimentation-based policy cycle" denotes the experimental efforts by local policymakers under the patronage of senior leaders, an important political mechanism of the central government to set local competition in motion but keep local practices at bay (Göbel 2011, Heilmann and Perry 2011).

While this is not the place to debate whether decentralization or centralization prevails, it should be fair to give credits to both camps because they all catch the seemingly paradoxical coexistence of central control and local variation as a defining feature of the Chinese politics. Recent works have recognized the limit of this dualistic conceptualization and proposed integral frameworks to encompass the salient Chinese style of decentralization (Chien 2007, Zheng 2007, Li 2010). These studies convey the key message of going beyond the dualist perspective that tends to overstress the antagonism between centre and locale while neglecting other possible cooperative interactions conducive to policy coordination. A better approach to the intergovernmental relations should thus incorporate the common values shared, or conflicting interests pursued, by both sides in their endeavours to achieve policy goals.

Compared to the robust research on the central–local relations and their roles in economic and fiscal policies, surprisingly scant attention has been paid to the impact of these political transformations on social policy.[1] Whereas political scientists focus mainly on the processes of economic and fiscal decentralization, scholars of Chinese social policy tend to put their analytical locus on the national level (i.e. central government). This research gap has resulted in the inability of both streams to offer an adequate account of the rising local social activism in recent decades. The preoccupation with economic or fiscal decentralization has left open the question about the rationales behind, and the way in which, local cadres' engagements with the relevant institutional innovation in social security. Meanwhile, the lopsided focus on social policy as dictated by the central government has equally overlooked the dimension of variegated local circumstances for policy transposition. Of great importance is to analyse how central and local governments interact to provide public goods in their bid to build a harmonious society.

To fill this gap, this article offers a theoretical perspective highlighting important aspects pertinent to the rise of decentralized social policy development in China. These include, first, the predominant role of local governments in the administration and finance of local social security programmes; second, central–local interactions in their attempts to promote economic growth and social stability; and finally, the governance challenge arising from the intergovernmental structures. Two concepts are proposed here: "social decentralization" to characterize the Chinese style of decentralized social security and "competitive solidarity" to stress the competitive logic inherent in Chinese policymaking processes. These two ideas are supposed to serve as a thought experiment in the hope to push forward our understanding of current developments in China's social policy. They are open to further examination in future studies.[2]

The next section discusses the idea of social decentralization in understanding the emergence of local social policy. The penultimate section further explores various important aspects of social decentralization, extending the concept of competitive solidarity to capture the competitive nature of localized social protection inherent in China's welfare system. The final section concludes these theoretical discussions and elaborates on their implications for further research on Chinese social policy.

Understanding social decentralization in China

This article proposes the concept "social decentralization" with reference to the emerging phenomenon of financial and administrative devotion in social security. In the Chinese context, this term entails two types of meaning: either the shifting responsibilities of welfare provision from the state onto the shoulders of the enterprises and individuals, or the reassignment of administrative jurisdiction between the central and local governments (Litvack et al. 1998; Rodriguez-Pose and Gill 2003). The first strand of research pays attention to the development of China's social policy in the transition from socialist to pluralist welfare production (cf. Saich 2008, Leung and Xu 2015, Ngok and Chan 2016). While the state sheds the burden of welfare provision to other societal sectors such as markets and families, the principle of egalitarian distribution stressed by the socialist regime has given way to other mechanisms that emphasized competition and efficiency. Even to date, reforms in various policy domains such as the health care have aroused heated debates about the adequate boundaries between the market mechanism and state administration (Duckett 2011). The commodification of labour and the marketization of welfare provision have led to increasing social inequality.

The other strand of social decentralization that is gaining in significance has, however, received less attention (cf. Frazier 2010, Carrillo and Duckett 2011, Shi 2012a, Ngok 2013). Much akin to the rise of economic and fiscal decentralization, both in urban and rural social security, or in some localities where urban–rural harmonization takes hold, local governments have gained greater competence for devising and financing a wide array of social security programmes to meet local welfare needs. Since 1978, there has been a continued trend of financial and administrative decentralization in the provision of public goods and welfare benefits. Particularly in recent decades, this Chinese style of "policy learning from within" has been characterized by various local experiments that have advanced the knowledge and practice of social policymaking; some of which with the delegation from the centre while others on the localities' own initiatives. Given the pivotal role of local governments in substantiating the regional social programmes, local variety of economic development and social provision is also arising as a conspicuous phenomenon.

Several factors account for the emergence of social decentralization. Given China's vast size and regional heterogeneity, reliance on local governments to carry out the welfare ends on site has resulted from necessity. Indeed, historical antecedents abound, even in the Maoist era (and the earlier revolutionary era) the idea and practice of local self-reliance persisted except several interruptions of political movements (Saich 2008, Heilmann and Perry 2011). The economic reforms since 1978 have altered the intergovernmental relations in ways that emphasize the principle of implementation according to local circumstances, with local governments gaining greater autonomy in economic development but also heavier burden for social provision. Local developmentalism has become the doctrine of the reform era, generating an imperative for local cadres to promote regional economic growth within their jurisdictions.

In tandem with the economic decentralization has been the direct personnel control of local cadres by the central government. Political accountability within this system is directed upwards to the upper echelon of government as local cadres' performances are evaluated upon a set of targets assigned from above. Such a "rule of mandates", that is, achievement-oriented and merit-based personnel policy, has succeeded in activating regional competition in favour of economic growth (Birney 2014). Indeed, the asymmetric combination of economic decentralization and political centralization has created strong incentives for local cadres to bring about effective strategies promoting economic development at the local level, contributing to the overall success of the economic reform in China (Walder 1995, Oi 1999, Whiting 2001, Chien 2007). This behavioural steering of local cadres by central command has also an important bearing on social policy. An effective tool of the latter is to set the social policy target and evaluate local cadres' performance upon a set of indicators (Landry 2008). Notable examples of this kind are directives of the central government since 2003 that required local governments to establish the basic rural pension insurance and cooperative healthcare systems. In this way, central leaders hold the reins on the extent of local policy implementation.

This tendency of local diversification gained further thrust with the socialist style of social security arrangements, whereby risk pooling in urban social insurance was designed at the city district or county level while rural social provision organized by villages. In urban and rural areas alike, ground-level government tiers took charge of welfare responsibilities throughout the period of planned economy. Although the economic reforms since 1978 have completely dismantled the socialist welfare arrangements towards a pluralized landscape of urban social insurance expanded to cover more population groups, together with the introduction of basic pension insurance and cooperative health care for rural peasants, the fundamental logic of local financing and administration has persisted until to date. Especially the fiscal decentralization since the "tax-assignment" reform of 1994 has shifted a large proportion of financial responsibility for social provision onto the shoulders of local governments. For lower government tiers, rising expenditure assignments are unmatched by declining revenue sharing, which places heavy financial burdens on local governments (Huang 1996, Wong and Bird 2008, Ngok 2013). For wealthy regions, the revenue relocation may be annoying but not fatal since they still have more budgets at disposal. For their poor counterparts, by contrast, fiscal reforms have snatched a critical amount of monetary resources away from the local pockets, causing financial difficulties especially at the lower government tiers. Although central government makes ad hoc financial transfers, there is no clear rule regulating the distribution of the centrally managed interregional redistribution.

Against the backdrop of economic and fiscal decentralization, social policy has become an essential element of the regional developmental strategies. Local leaders are obliged to search out an adequate combination of promoting economic growth and maintaining social stability – an essential political merit facilitative of personal career. This is at times no easy task as some social security programmes may be resource-consuming, for example, the case of pensions clearly absorb fiscal budgets away that could have been mobilized for boosting further economic development. Local developmentalism further poses constraints on the extent of social policy expansion because each region has to compete for inward investment and tends to depress local wages or social insurance contributions to enhance the appeal of the location for business. In the meantime, local cadres face the pressures from the centre or upper government echelons to implement social security measures that may not entirely lie in the local interest. Reconciling the at times contradicting interests has become a key issue in local social policy governance.

Social decentralization and competitive solidarity

The specific context of Chinese-style developmental path is an important frame of reference for capturing the essence of China's social policy. To some extent, the latter's developments are analogous to those occurring in the European Union (EU) social policy. In the course of European integration, welfare sovereignty of the member states has been gradually eroded by the market force of a single European Economic Community and the corresponding supranational intervention of the EU, leading to unbalanced situation of a rising single European market without counterweight, that is, the lack of a parallel supranational regulatory framework at the EU level to mitigate the negative consequences of market liberalization (Scharpf 1999, Leibfried 2010). With the deepening integration, however, the EU is beginning to influence the welfare politics of its member states: starting with the social insurance coordination for migrant workers to facilitate free movement of persons during the 1970s, the community has ever since extended its jurisdictions to core welfare spheres such as health care and pensions (Eckardt 2005, Ferrera 2005).

In recent waves of globalization, however, integration of the European social policy has gradually come to piecemeal progress. "Competitive solidarity" is a term that first appears in the literature to characterize the changing dynamics of the EU social policy. In his remarks on the relationship between national welfare states and European integration, Streeck (2000, p. 252) notes:

> In trying to adapt to the new economic circumstances, national communities seek to defend their solidarity, less through protection and redistribution than through *joint competitive and productive success* – through politics, not *against* markets, but *within* and *with* them, gradually replacing *protective* and *redistributive* with *competitive* and *productive* solidarity. (Italics in original)

Competitive solidarity characterizes the turn of EU social policy from emphasizing redistribution based on social justice to enhancing human capital based on economic competitiveness. The key message underlying this idea is the rebranding of the European social model towards the "productivist reconstruction of solidarity" (Streeck 2000, 259). The intensified competition in the process of globalization and, above all, European single-market project has put member states and their subordinate regions under pressures to dismantle the existing social security programmes, while efforts to rebuild centrally coordinated redistribution at the European level remain largely incomplete. In this process, central governments of large countries fail to satisfy the specific productive requirements of the heterogeneous regions with different economic sectors. Political federalism has thus risen to prominence especially in recent decades, partly out of the growing subnational identities but also in response to the imperative for sectoral specialization. The consequence has been the rising regionalization alongside the trend towards globalization and Europeanization. Solidarity in Europe remains nationally (or regionally) confined despite decades of integrative efforts by the elites to bring forth "ever closer union". This happens just when growing competition among the member states or regions is in need of supranational coordination, though the latter seems unable to live up to this expectation due to the EU's institutional design that contains the extent of supranational expansion. Competitive solidarity reveals much about the dilemma between the keen competition among the "parts" that tends to intensify regional inequality and the growing need for the intricate coordination task of the "whole" from above to mitigate the adverse effects of the market integration. Both are hard to reconcile with each other.

These difficulties associated with the turn towards "competitive solidarity" in the EU bear some resemblance to the case of China's social policy. In its embrace of globalization, China's economic growth in the 1980s and 1990s has been, by and large, premised on the competitive logic of local developmentalism in its bid to build a business-friendly environment that can accommodate the market requirements. The preoccupation with economic development has been reinforced by the personnel evaluation of the ruling Communist party that lay emphasis on the GDP-ism, thus motivating local cadres to pursue regional development at all prices – often to the detriment of people's welfare needs within their jurisdictions, such as poor labour conditions and social insecurity for the marginalized groups. In brief, the essence of developmentalism inherent in China's local governance is from its outset little to do with protective and redistributive, but rather about competitive and productive in nature. Three aspects stand out to highlight these features: regional competition, local protectionism and central coordination of local policy implementation.

Regional competition and emulation

The parallel development of economic decentralization and political centralization in the first two decades since economic reforms has unleashed regional competition, setting local governments to vie with one another in the quest for capital and other resources (Edin 2003, Landry 2008). During this period, social security used to be regarded as a grave burden on the local finance, producing a disincentive for local governments to expand local social programmes unless otherwise dictated by the central government. Efforts to canvass inward investment have generated downward pressures on wages and the associated labour costs, reflected in the concessions that local governments often had to make in labour standards or tax exemptions. Local non-compliance or lag in transposition were thus common practices that have often undermined the efficacy of social policy. The lack of democratic accountability further weakened the readiness of local cadres to address the real concerns of their people. The balance between economic and social policies was clearly tilted towards the former at the expense of the latter.

Not all social policies delivered merely disadvantages, though. Under some circumstances, social policy might yield its benefits when local governments discovered the advantage of garnering subsidies from the central government. Indeed, since the 1990s local pilot experimentation has become an essential locomotive of social policy learning conducive to innovative or even groundbreaking policy options (Shi 2012a). Behind local social initiatives often stood the authorization from the central ministries that encouraged selected localities to embark on pilot schemes probing with new policy ideas and frameworks. During the reforms of urban pension and health insurances, pilot policy experimentation has essentially contributed to the accumulation of knowledge that framed the subsequent policy guidelines of the central government.

Meanwhile, local governments in well-off regions also took initiatives in local social policies in the quest for adequate solutions in response to new social problems resulting from rapid industrialization and urbanization. Particularly here local social activism has played an important part in recent policy innovation, also thanks to the steady local finance that made heavy subsidies of the new pilot schemes possible. Not coincidentally, the introduction of the Minimum Living Standard Scheme or the Township Insurance Scheme for landless peasants all took place in Shanghai during the 1990s, in part because the leading coastal city had to tackle the problems of urban poverty or land expropriation (Shang and Wu 2004, Chan 2010). The active social experimentation at the local level has gained further momentum since the 2000s as the central leaders encouraged local governments to take efficacious measures for building a "harmonious society". Numerous local pilot initiatives have sprouted ever since, notably the experimentation with urban–rural harmonization in Chengdu since 2003, followed by the later recognition of the central government in 2007 that authorized Chengdu (together with Chongqing) the formal status of experimentation zone for this new welfare engineering (Shi 2012b). Various approaches led by Chengdu and other localities to urban–rural harmonization have provided the ground for the new Xi-Li leadership to announce even larger scale of urbanization, despite Xi's recent purge of Chengdu's and Chongqing's leading cadres.

Moreover, with the coastal regions gradually reaching a critical threshold of economic growth, successive efforts have been underway on the part of local governments to refurbish local industrial structures by demanding higher social policy calibres. A good example was the raising of minimum wages and labour protection standards in many coastal regions in the wake of the financial crisis of 2008 (Chan and Nadvi 2014). Partly upon the command of the central government, but more out of the contemplation to restructure the local economies, social policy has been utilized as a strategy to enforce the industrial upgrading – with discernible consequences (Hong 2014, Brandt and Thun 2016). The emigration of labour-intensive industries in the Pearl River Delta to the Western inland or even Southeast Asia has occupied wide media coverage. Particularly the move of labour-intensive industries towards Western China merits close attention since it signals a reshuffling process of successive industrialization at the regional scale, with Western backward inland following the lead of Eastern coastal regions in the path towards economic growth. This widening regional gap in terms of economic growth and social provision implies that it would be more adequate to examine the economic and social patterns of regions with about the same developmental level. It is very likely that the roles of social policy among regions with different economic levels may vary, depending on the context of local developments.

This is particularly the case for those inland regions whose economies are currently improving, and yet face diverse political and social constraints. Moderate public financial strength and limited central fiscal transfers confine the local governments' leeway for benefit generosity in a time when the demand for social security among local residents is rising. For example, Henan and Sichuan are populous provinces with large labour outflows, implying certain disadvantage for the finance of local social security programmes since a considerable proportion of the remaining insured persons are those very likely to claim benefits, such as the elderly. Under these circumstances, inland local cadres tend to follow the strategies of their colleagues of the rich coastal regions to widen the coverage of the existing social security programmes but limit the benefit provision to merely affordable levels (Huang 2015). Depending on local circumstances, local governments have various rationales to extend/withhold social security to different population groups.

Regional protectionism

A further feature of the competitive solidarity in China relates to the welfare exclusivism of local social security programmes. Initially in the pre-reform era, the rigid household registration (*hukou*) divided China's social security system into two separate worlds of social citizenship, namely an employment-based comprehensive social insurance system for urban residents and a community-based residual social assistance system for rural population. With the ban on rural–urban mobility gradually loosened since the 1980s, a large flow of rural peasants has migrated into cities in search of better lives. Numerous research works have documented that, although migrant workers constituted the major source of cheap labour supply especially for coastal regions that were keen to develop local economies, the latter raised huge barricades for the migrants' access to local welfare benefits (Solinger 1999, Nielsen and Smyth 2008, Wu 2010). The incipient local policy experiments introduced a separate insurance programme with inferior protection for this specific group, later amended by recent initiatives to grant the employed migrants access to the urban worker social insurance. However, in the absence of clear central directives to offer concrete policy frameworks, local approaches towards the floating population remain diverse.

Only in the last few years did the central government demonstrate resolution of "deepening reforms" by ordering local governments to eliminate administrative barrier for the floating population. In 2014, the State Department issued the "Opinion on further *Hukou* Reform" proclaiming the abolition of the "agricultural/non-agricultural (i.e. urban–rural)" divide in the household registration system. This document manifested the intention to ease the restriction imposed upon the migrant workers in access to welfare benefits of the residing cities. Following this move, the central government declared in 2015 the "Provisional Arrangement of Residence Document" (*juzhuzheng zhanxing tiaoli*) stipulating that all citizens who have been inhabiting and working in a borough for over 6 months are entitled to its compulsory education and elementary public services.[3] However, this policy progress should be counterbalanced by the fact that granting access to these local benefits is far from the acquisition of local *hukou* status which sets strict criteria for the applicants. Especially metropolises such as Beijing, Guangzhou, Shenzhen and Shanghai remain stringent in this regard. Only middle- or small-sized cities have opened their gates with little reservation to rural migrants.

In broader sense, the defensive stance of local governments to prevent outsiders from sharing the benefits of social security programmes results from the decentralized nature of social provision. Despite gradual loosening of the *hukou* system, especially wealthy regions still preserve differential status categories for interregional migration control on the grounds of capacity limit in local finance (cf. Chan and Buckingham 2008, Wu 2010). This applies also to the case of recent efforts by well-off regions to harmonize their own social security programmes in order to eliminate the urban–rural divide in social protection. As local social activism is gaining strength, local social programmes are also growing in significance to categorize the social rights of residents within their respective jurisdictions (Shi 2012b). The tight link between welfare entitlements and local resident status (*hukou*) gives rise to local protectionist barriers that exclude outsiders (urban and rural alike) from claiming local social benefits because the latter are almost solely financed by local budgets. Social security reforms of recent years have ameliorated this discrimination by allowing migrant workers to join the contributory social insurance programmes such as pension and healthcare insurances, part of whose benefits are portable nationwide in case the insured workers move elsewhere. By contrast, non-contributory welfare entitlements such as local social assistance remain reserved for residents only.[4]

The exclusive nature of local social programmes towards "welfare tourism" of outsiders has its institutional foundation, namely the fragmented administrative and financial structures of social security institutions. As noted above, already in the pre-reform era, both urban social insurance for workers and rural programmes for peasants were largely financed by local governments (counties and township, respectively) (Ngok 2013, Dillon 2015). This basic financial and administrative principle has persisted throughout the reform era despite recent attempts to upgrade the administrative level of risk pooling and funding redistribution in urban social insurance. Especially in the urban pension reforms of the 1990s, the central government has been keen to widen the risk pools in a bid to overcome the institutional fragmentation – at the price of huge financial concessions made by the centre to cover the deficits in local insurance finance. The pilot schemes implemented in the Liaoning province and other northeastern provinces since the 2000s is one notable example, whereby the central government poured a large number of subsidies to assist these rustbelt industrial provinces in filling the empty pension accounts of the urban workers. Even to date, this task is far from accomplished, as in many places the pooling levels remain at the county level. Without the necessary institutional integration, each locality would still bear the main financial responsibility – and in the case of well-off regions, local governments would tend to preserve financial surpluses for own discretion without any incentive to share them with other localities.

Central coordination and local implementation in social security

Together with economic and financial decentralization, the trend towards decentralized social provision has motivated local governments to establish regional social security programmes complementary to own development strategies, or even probe for new programmatic directions to tackle social problems. Especially in the new millennium, new ideas such as "take humanity as basis" (*yiren weiben*) or "inclusive growth" (*baorongxing zengzhang*) came to the fore, manifesting the growing awareness of the party-state about social protection as an essential complement for the market economy (Gong and Su 2010). Many localities have launched various pilot schemes to explore approaches aimed at eliminating discriminatory treatment of residents with different household registration status (*hukou*) for entitlements to social benefits. These harmonization efforts are set to influence the next stage of social security reform, with local governments undoubtedly playing a crucial role as the propeller of local experimentation.

Meanwhile, in its quest for "deepening reform", the current central leaders are also advocating a further step towards "urbanization", aiming to achieve a more integral approach of regional development well beyond the traditional dualism of urban-rural divide. To achieve this goal, central government turns to the powerful "magic wand" of personnel evaluation mechanism to steer local cadres' priority in local policy agenda. By assigning more weight to guidelines and indicators about social welfare in the cadre performance evaluation, this will exert binding effects on the welfare-oriented policies at local level as they are bundled with career promotion of cadres. Empirical analysis has shown a marked shift towards welfarism in municipal policy implementation after 2006 in response to Beijing's emphasis on better people's livelihood and social policy. Especially for mayors, generally the second-rank local leaders, the incentives to promote social policy and stability are strong (Smith 2013, Zuo 2015). Some provinces such as Jiangxi even introduced monetary measures (bonus) to reward local cadres who delivered excellent performances in carrying out necessary healthcare reforms.[5]

The growing significance of local social activism has an important bearing on the social policy development in China as it sets in motion dynamic institutional changes in favour of the welfare "regions" rather than the welfare "state" (Shi 2012a). The regionalization of social protection poses both advantages and disadvantages. Given China's vast size and regional heterogeneity, social decentralization results from necessity since local governments have to devise appropriate social programmes to accommodate specific regional diversity. The central government, for its part, is also wise not to meddle too much in the local administration of social security affairs as long as social stability at the local level is maintained. In this way, central leaders can comfortably place the responsibilities for welfare provision on the shoulders of their local cadres. The rising social policy initiatives have also contributed to social policy innovation in China. In many subdomains of social policy, the central government has been effectively activating local experimentation conducive to new social policy designs. Here the former also relies on local experiences with new policy ideas to gather valuable lessons for issuing nationwide policy guidelines.

Although flexible local discretion has facilitated policy innovation, diverse local experimentation often generates a wide variety of institutional designs that render subsequent coordination or integration by the centre enormously difficult. Often various local programmes with diverse financial methods (pay-as-you-go or fully funded) make it extremely arduous to integrate. Examples of the kind abound during the social security reforms such as the urban and rural pension reforms of the 1990s (Béland and Yu 2004, Frazier 2010, Shi 2011). In the former case, various pilot schemes implemented at different localities posed enormous difficulties for the central government in its later efforts to upgrade the financial pooling at the upper government echelons such as the provinces or prefectures since rich localities with financial strength had tended to resist the integration attempts that required them to share the financial surpluses with other poorer counterparts. It took the central government great pains, not least by means of huge financial concessions, to achieve this goal. In the latter case, rural pension reforms have undergone turbulent processes during the 1990s, as local implementation wobbled to such an extent that the central government decided to halt the ongoing programmes and replaced them with an entirely new policy approach in 2003.

Given the widening regional disparities in terms of financial strength and administrative capacity, the only possible convergence dictated by the central government is to erect a basic pillar of social security with universal coverage and need-based entitlements (*guangfugai, dishuiping*), to which supplementary schemes can be established according to local circumstances (*duocengci*), while equally securing their long-term financial sustainability (*kechixu*). This leitmotif characterizes the essence of Chinese social security reforms in the new millennium. One recent example is the "Insurance of Critical Illness" (*dabing baoxian*), introduced in 2015 as an extension (and revision) of the existing Basic Health Insurance for Urban and Rural Residents that failed in the past to offer sufficient protection for the insured persons with grave illness.[6] So far, local pilot schemes of 31 provinces and autonomous regions are underway after the State Council issued an opinion requiring local action in this regard. Its basic idea is to provide financial subsidies to the insured persons proportional to their medical expenses. Depending on their fiscal conditions, local governments are free to top up the range of subsidies, though at least 50% of the incurred disbursements must be covered. One such policy design ensures nationwide basic protection and allows room for further local social activism.

Since each locality is predicated to search out its own approach to promoting economic growth while providing social security to the inhabitants within its own jurisdiction, well-off regions with steady financial strength tend to devise local welfare programmes specifically addressing the needs of local residents. These programmes usually supplement the basic programmes but offer better social protection or higher welfare benefits. These circumstances offer fertile soil for a multi-speed institutional evolution in China's social policy, in which well-off regions establish local welfare programmes at a fast pace, followed by the rest of the country that has to manage reasonable social policy expansion while keeping local economic prospect or fiscal capacity aloft. The regionalization of social protection is transforming China's social security into a garden variety of social programmes that take on basic institutional contours as stipulated by the central government, but diverge in substances in terms of benefit levels and financial methods.

Conclusion: social decentralization, Chinese style

China's fast economic growth in the past decades has been achieved by the central government's strategy to set regional competition in motion, entrenching an inherent competitive milieu prompting each region's endeavours for development, whether promoting economic growth, strengthening environmental protection or even improving social security. In the meantime, social security is gaining weight in public perception that requires more state involvement in social provision. In their bid to stimulate regional growth, local cadres have to strike the delicate balance between the imperative for economic development and the public quest (or central command) for social protection. As such, social policy is subject to the interplay of various logics: the political imperative by dint of cadre evaluation of the Communist party, the economic doctrine with emphasis on local developments and the social demand to maintain collective stability.

Meanwhile, regionalization of social protection is also setting the regions under pressure to vie with their peers not only in economic performance but also for social protection. Competitive solidarity refers to the configurations of welfare regions in competition with one another, with each devising its own welfare model that caters, first and foremost, to specific local circumstances while precluding outsiders from sharing the welfare benefits. Social solidarity in China thus takes on a strong territorial character, implying less about nationwide income redistribution and overarching social egalitarianism than about interregional contest for development and mutual exclusion of social citizenship. The common denominator stipulated by central government to overcome the inherent heterogeneity among regional social security is to set a national minimum benchmark for benefit levels (e.g. basic pensions in the Urban/Rural Resident Pension Insurance), often financed by central budgets. In addition, the central government has turned to the problem of regional disparities in recent years by providing subsidies to poor regions based on individual welfare programmes, which helps narrow the extent of regional inequality in social protection. However, central initiatives of this scale can hardly countervail the centrifugal force of regional competition that breeds the regional disparities. A much larger scale of interregional monetary transfers would be needed to mitigate the regional gaps in developmental levels.

All these developments point to the necessity to take heed of the institutional dynamics currently undergoing in China's regional social policy. Particularly under the new Xi-Li leadership, when the central government is striving to reconfigure the overall economic structures with the idea of "supply-side reforms" (*gongjice gaige*). In its essence lies the attempt to redress the shortcomings of the past approaches reliant on overinvestment and overproduction at the expense of notorious labour conditions and serious environmental pollution. Motors of future economic growth should shift from carrying on export-led industrialization to boosting domestic consumption.[7] As one of the major catalysts for "deepening reforms", the new reform idea clearly suggests that social security will play a significant role in helping the households avert major life risks in the post-socialist economy, thereby strengthening their ability to increase consumption with their savings. The prospect of social policy expansion is very likely to consolidate the logic of competitive solidarity inherent in social decentralization as the present study analyses. While the role of central government in policymaking and coordination remains dominant in social policy, social decentralization has clearly hoisted local governments to become a perhaps even more critical figure in setting the local landscape of social security. The complex interactions between central–local and among local governments also call attention to the specific style of competitive solidarity that shapes the patterns of competition, coordination, learning and diffusion.

Notes

1. Only recently have some scholars noticed this theme. See Carrillo and Duckett (2011), Hussain (2007), Shi (2012a) and Ngok (2013).
2. The author is grateful for the constructive criticism of one reviewer about the applicability of these concepts. The main idea here is to draw attention to similar, if not identical, developments happening in the West where decentralization is also an important issue. See e.g. McEwen and Moreno (2005); Béland and Lecours (2008).
3. http://www.gov.cn/zhengce/content/2015-12/12/content_10398.htm; accessed 5 February 2016.
4. The author is indebted to one reviewer for reminding this point.

5. General Office of Jiangxi Provincial Government. 16 November, 2015, 'Implementation opinion on the performance evaluation and assessment of healthcare reforms in 2015'. Available at: http://www.jxwst.gov.cn/cszw/tzgg/ddyjc/201511/t20151117_409146.htm, accessed on 4 July 2016.
6. Information on the Insurance of Critical Illness is retrieved from the Chinese government website: http://big5.gov.cn/gate/big5/www.gov.cn/zhengce/2015-08/03/content_2907667.htm.
7. Xinhua Net News: *Supply-side Reform to Keep Chinese Economy Fit.* 4 January 2016. Accessed at: http://news.xinhuanet.com/english/2016-01/04/c_134977011.htm.

Acknowledgements

An earlier draft of this article was presented at the joint conference of SPA and EASP at the University of York, UK, July 2012. Thanks to Professor Shiuh-Shen Chien, Drs Chung-min Tsai, Chih-shian Liou, I-Chieh Fang for their valuable comments. This work was supported by the Ministry of Science and Technology, Taiwan [NSC 102-2410-H-002-089-MY2].

Disclosure statement

No potential conflict of interest was reported by the author.

Funding

This work was supported by the Ministry of Science and Technology, Taiwan [NSC 102-2410-H-002-089-MY2].

References

Béland, D. and Yu, K.M., 2004. A long financial march: pension reform in China. *Journal of Social Policy*, 33 (2), 267–288. doi:10.1017/S004727940300744X

Béland, D. and Lecours, A., 2008. *Nationalism and social policy: the politics of territorial solidarity*. Oxford: Oxford University Press.

Birney, M., 2014. Decentralization and veiled corruption under China's "rule of mandates". *World Development*, 53, 55–67. doi:10.1016/j.worlddev.2013.01.006

Brandt, L. and Thun, E., 2016. Constructing a ladder for growth: policy, markets, and industrial upgrading in China. *World Development*, 80 (April), 78–95. doi:10.1016/j.worlddev.2015.11.001

Cai, H. and Treisman, D., 2006. Did government decentralisation cause China's economic miracle? *World Politics*, 58 (7), 505–535. doi:10.1353/wp.2007.0005

Cao, Y., Qian, Y., and Weingast, B., 1999. From federalism, Chinese style to privatisation, Chinese style. *Economics of Transition*, 7 (1), 103–131. doi:10.1111/1468-0351.00006

Carrillo, B. and Duckett, J., eds, 2011. *China's changing welfare mix: local perspectives*. London: Routledge.

Chan, C.K., 2010. Re-thinking the incrementalist thesis in China: a reflection on the development of the minimum standard of living scheme in urban and rural areas. *Journal of Social Policy*, 39 (4), 627–645. doi:10.1017/S0047279410000322

Chan, -C.K.-C. and Nadvi, K., 2014. Changing labour regulations and labour standards in China: retrospect and challenges. *International Labour Review*, 153 (4), 513–534. doi:10.1111/j.1564-913X.2014.00214.x

Chan, K.W. and Buckingham, W., 2008. Is China abolishing the Hukou system? *China Quarterly*, 195, 582–606.

Chien, -S.-S., 2007. Institutional innovations, asymmetric decentralisation and local economic development – case study of Kunshan in post-Mao China. *Environment and Planning C: Government and Policy*, 25 (2), 269–290. doi:10.1068/c0558

Dillon, N., 2015. *Radical inequalities: China's revolutionary welfare state in comparative perspective*. Cambridge, MA: Harvard University Press.

Duckett, J., 2011. *The Chinese state's retreat from health: policy and the politics of retrenchment*. London: Routledge.

Eckardt, M., 2005. The open method of coordination on pensions: an economic analysis of its effects on pension reforms. *Journal of European Social Policy*, 15 (3), 247–267. doi:10.1177/0958928705054088

Edin, M., 2003. State capacity and local agent control in China: CCP cadre management from a township perspective. *The China Quarterly*, 173, 35–52. doi:10.1017/S0009443903000044

Ferrera, M., 2005. *The boundaries of welfare: European integration and the new spatial politics of social protection*. Oxford: Oxford University Press.

Frazier, M.W., 2010. *Socialist insecurity: pensions and the politics of uneven development in China*. Ithaca: Cornell University Press.

Göbel, C., 2011. Uneven policy implementation in rural China. *The China Journal*, 65, 53–76. doi:10.1086/tcj.65.25790557

Gong, S. and Su, Y., 2010. *Social policies for both people's livelihood and inclusive growth*. Beijing: Social Sciences Academic Press (in Chinese).

Heilmann, S. and Perry, E.J., 2011. *Mao's invisible hand: the political foundations of adaptative governance in China*. Cambridge, MA: Harvard University Press.

Hong, Y., 2014. Industrial upgrading in Guangdong: how well is it performing? *China: an International Journal*, 12 (1), 108–131.

Huang, X., 2015. Four worlds of welfare: understanding subnational variation in Chinese social health insurance. *The China Quarterly*, 222, 449–474. doi:10.1017/S0305741015000399

Huang, Y., 1996. Central-local relations in China during the reform era: the economic and institutional dimensions. *World Development*, 24 (4), 655–672.

Hussain, A., 2007. Setting up an integrated social security system. *China Perspectives*, 3, 92–98.

Landry, P.F., 2008. *Decentralized authoritarianism in China: the communist party's control of local elites in the post-Mao era*. Cambridge: Cambridge University Press.

Leibfried, S., 2010. Social policy: left to the judges and the markets? In: H. Wallace, W. Wallace, and M.A. Pollack, eds. *Policy-making in the European Union*. Oxford: Oxford University Press, 253–281.

Leung, J.C.B. and Xu, Y., 2015. *China's social welfare: the third turning point*. Hoboken: John Wiley & Sons.

Li, L.C., 2010. Central-local relations in the People's Republic of China: trends, processes and impacts for policy implementation. *Public Administration and Development*, 30, 177–190.

Litvack, J., et al., 1998. *Rethinking decentralisation in developing countries*. Washington: World Bank.

McEwen, N. and Moreno, L., eds, 2005. *The territorial politics of welfare*. London: Routledge.

Mertha, A., 2005. China's soft centralisation: shifting Tiao/Kuai authority relations. *China Quarterly*, 184, 791–810.

Montinola, G., Qian, Y., and Weingast, B., 1995. Federalism, Chinese style: the political basis for economic success in China. *World Politics*, 48 (10), 50–81.

Ngok, K., 2013. Recent social policy expansion and its implications for intergovernmental financial relations in China. *Australian Journal of Public Administration*, 72 (3), 344–358.

Ngok, K. and Chan, K.C., eds, 2016. *China's social policy: transformation and challenges*. Abingdon: Routledge.

Nielsen, I. and Smyth, R., eds, 2008. *Migration and social protection in China*. Singapore: World Scientific Publishing.

Oi, J.C., 1999. *Rural China takes off: institutional foundations of economic reform*. Berkeley: University of California Press.

Rodriguez-Pose, A. and Gill, N., 2003. The global trend towards devolution and its implications. *Environment and Planning C: Government and Policy*, 21 (3), 333–351.

Saich, T., 2008. *Providing public goods in transitional China*. New York: Palgrave Macmillan.

Shang, X. and Wu, X., 2004. Changing approaches of social protection: social assistance reform in urban China. *Social Policy & Society*, 3 (3), 259–271.

Scharpf, F., 1999. *Governing in Europe: effective and democratic?* Oxford: Oxford University Press.

Shi, S.-J., 2011. The contesting quest for old-age security: institutional politics in China's pension reforms. *Journal of Asian Public Policy*, 4 (1), 42–60.

Shi, S.-J., 2012a. Social policy learning and diffusion in China: the rise of welfare regions? *Policy & Politics*, 40 (3), 367–385.

Shi, S.-J., 2012b. Towards inclusive social citizenship? Rethinking China's social security in the trend towards urban-rural harmonisation. *Journal of Social Policy*, 41 (4), 789–810.

Smith, G., 2010. The hollow state: rural governance in China. *China Quarterly*, 203, 601–618.

Smith, G., 2013. Measurement, promotions and patterns of behavior in Chinese local government. *The Journal of Peasant Studies*, 40 (6), 1027–1050.

Solinger, D.J., 1999. *Contesting citizenship in urban China: peasant migrants, the state, and the logic of the market*. Berkeley: University of California Press.

Streeck, W., 2000. Competitive solidarity: rethinking the European social model. *In*: K. Hinrichs, H. Kitschelt, and H. Wiesenthal, eds. *Kontingenz und Krise: Institutionenpolitik in kapitalistischen und postsozialistischen Gesellschaften*. Frankfurt: Campus Verlag, 245–261.

Walder, A.G., 1995. Local governments as industrial firms: an organisational analysis of China's transitional economy. *American Journal of Sociology*, 101 (2), 263–301.

Whiting, S.H., 2001. *Power and wealth in rural China: the political economy of institutional change*. Cambridge: Cambridge University Press.

Wong, C.P.W. and Bird, R.M., 2008. China's fiscal system: a work in progress. *In*: L. Brandt and T.G. Rawski, eds. *China's great economic transformation*. Cambridge: Cambridge University Press, 429–466.

Wu, J.-M., 2010. Rural migrant workers and China's differential citizenship: a comparative institutional analysis. *In*: M.K. Whyte, ed. *One country, two societies: rural-urban inequality in contemporary China*. Cambridge, MA: Harvard University Press, 55–81.

Zhao, L. and Lim, T.S., eds, 2010. *China's new social policy: initiatives for a harmonious society*. Singapore: World Scientific Publishing.

Zheng, Y., 2007. *De facto federalism in China: reforms and dynamics of central-local relations*. Singapore: World Scientific Publishing.

Zuo, C.V., 2015. Promoting city leaders: the structure of political incentives in China. *The China Quarterly*, 224, 955–984.

RESEARCH ARTICLE

East Asian welfare regime: obsolete ideal-type or diversified reality

Peter Abrahamson

ABSTRACT
The paper asks if East Asian welfare regimes are still productivist and Confucian? And, have they developed public care policies? The literature is split on the first question but (mostly) confirmative on the second. Care has to a large, but insufficient extent, been rolled out in the region. Political science studies tend to conclude that the region has left the old legacies behind and are now welfare states comparable to European states including them either in the conservative type (e.g. Japan), the liberal type (e.g. Korea) or even as a tendency in the Nordic type (e.g. China), while studies focusing on outcomes or causal links tend to suggest that legacies prevail, but there is (nearly) consensus that Confucianism exercises great influence in the whole region.

Introduction

Within the so-called welfare modelling business (Abrahamson, 1999), there has been a growing interest to characterize East Asian states as belonging to a particular welfare regime. Three dimensions have been highlighted: they are productivist and developmental, they are Confucian and they are small spenders; but the literature has also pointed out that the regime approach, being statist, is ill suited to capture a region in which developments are very fast.

In an earlier paper, I suggested that East Asia indeed was a moving target, but that it could be described as an informal care regime by emphasizing its familistic character (Abrahamson, 2011). The literature on East Asian welfare regime during the 2000s had largely abandoned the Confucian label and since all welfare states can be characterized as productivist that label was also down played. Instead, the rapid development of social security and social services were emphasized; but development of personal social services in particular were seen as rudimentary; hence the big space for informal care services delivered within the family by female members.

This paper returns to the debate by considering the recent literature with a special focus on care and the results are quite surprising. There has been a revival of Catherine Jones Finer's now classic papers on 'Oiconomic welfare states' (1990) and 'Confucian welfare states' (1993) to the extent that these references now (again) have become mainstream. Furthermore, discussions have returned to the perspective of productivist and developmental and keeps insisting that social policies in East Asia in the main are subordinated economic development. By focusing on family policies such as parental leave, long-term care insurance (LTCI) and childcare the familistic and thus Confucian elements of the welfare regime are questioned.

The connection between development and expansion of care services is intimately linked with welfare regime characteristics because their introduction is motivated by increasing female labour force participation, which presupposes a better work-life balance and, hence a break with the Confucian elements where women are seen as the major carers of frail elderly, handicapped and disabled family members and their own children. As is well known, the current imbalance in East Asia has led to the world's lowest fertility and a rapid ageing of societies. Changes in care policies are meant to partially release women from their 'double' burden; but the take-up rate of for instance parental leave and paternity leave demonstrate how the persistence of Confucian values prohibits implementation because of resistance among employers and male family members.

Are the East Asian welfare regimes productivist?

To my mind, the most influential approach to welfare organization in East Asia are the ideas of productivist welfare state (Holiday 2000) and developmental welfare states (Kwon 2005). Despite their differences, both perspectives maintain that social policies are subordinated economic development resulting in small or lean welfare states. In these cases, welfare policies have the twin purpose of securing the support of core constituencies or appeasing potential political opposition and directly underpinning economic development, e.g. by providing a well-educated workforce through public education; hence, only core workers in strategic industries and public employees are included in the limited programmes that furthermore were contribution based. Such a perspective covers quite neatly the early development of the Japanese, South Korean and Taiwanese cases, and some observers of current welfare development stick to that perspective.

Hence, Hwang (2012) analysing Japan, Korea and Taiwan proposed that 'although there has been significant change made to social policy in the region, structural conditions and the politics of expansion associated with them are yet to amount to a shift in the core foundation of their welfare production logic. The market-conforming role of social policy in East Asia has been persistent'. A similar observation is made by Yang (2013) who is very critical of all the colleagues that attach significance to the apparent expansion of care policies in the region. He focuses on the small spender perspective and attributes some explanation to the productivist thesis. At the same time, he is critical of it because of its functionalism, 'Almost everything unique in the Korean welfare state is reduced to the functional prerequisites for economic development' (Yang 2013, p. 460). Yang maintains the developmental characteristic based on the lack of a labour movement and leftist political parties, which is viewed as a precondition for a welfare state.

Ahn and Lee (2012) tried to determine whether Korea with the political changes in the early 2000s had shifted from a developmental to a welfare state regime. They concluded that 'Findings suggest that Korean welfare state developed together with the increased needs from demographic changes in combination with economic development, while evidence for the effect of a left-oriented government or globalization on welfare state development is weak or not found' (Ahn and Lee 2012, p. 82).

Observations regarding the small city states of the region, Hong Kong, Macau and Singapore unanimously confine them to the productivist and developmental paradigm, despite more social policy investments (Mok 2013, Lai and Chui 2014). Illustrative is the work of Teo. She discussed recent welfare reforms in Singapore and starts out by comparing them to similar reforms in Japan, Korea and Hong Kong and acknowledges apparently similar developments of expanding social spending as reaction to changing demographic and economic conditions, communicated through political mobilization. But she is critical to viewing greater social spending and rhetorical attention to marginalized groups as indication of a change in policy logic. Through detailed analyses of welfare reforms, she 'shows that the Singapore state's claims of increased attention to spending and redistribution, to "equality" and "social inclusion" are limited in three ways, a strong orientation toward subsidizing companies; modest and conditional direct aid to low-income households; and a consistent and persistent neglect of the gendered inequalities in both care and wage work' (Teo 2015a, p. 96). Teo concluded Singapore to be a limited welfare state.

Not surprisingly, other studies support a change in regime paradigm away from productivist and developmental towards European style welfare states of either Conservative (Japan) Liberal (Korea and Taiwan) or even Social Democratic (China) orientation. Thus, Choi (2012) asks whether we are witnessing an 'End of the Era of Productivist Welfare Capitalism?' He analysed China, Japan and Korea, and found that Japan should still be considered a productivist welfare regime, but maintained 'that Korea is a welfare state regime with strong liberal characteristics via modern welfare politics'. Furthermore, 'Since the needs for social policy expansion in China correspond to economic and political needs, the productivist feature has been significantly weakened'. The overarching conclusion is that 'there are two strong signs that these states are moving out of their productivist nature and also that they are in the process of establishing their own welfare states' (Choi 2012, p. 275). Similar conclusions regarding Korea and Taiwan were reached by Kim and Shi (2013), 'To date, few would raise doubts as to whether the welfare state has been or is being institutionalized in South Korea and Taiwan .... In the face of economic globalization, both societies adopted social investment strategies such as activating labor markets and expanding child care in reaction to new social risks' (Kim and Shi 2013, p. 120).

Finally, I shall mention a comparative paper by Lin and Wong (2013) which is indicative of the paradigm shift perspective. They identified three policy orientations which they group into three models, the redistributive model, the productivist model, and the inclusive model, and they found a shift from the productive policy model towards the redistributive and inclusive ones when analysing the development in Japan, Korea, Mainland China, Taiwan, Singapore and Hong Kong. Lin & Wong argue that under the influence of structural changes in work and demography and democratization the countries in the region changed their social policy orientation, 'the ethos guiding social policy in this stage transits from residual productivist ideals to redistributive and inclusive ones' (Lin and Wong 2013, p. 278). Ideas of redistribution and social rights became widely accepted by the public and thus paved the way for a paradigm shift from productivist to a mix of that and a redistributive social policy model. 'Thus, a new set of policy ideas are adopted, including welfare rights, inclusiveness, social cohesion, redistribution, and social empowerment' (Lin and Wong 2013, p. 281).

Are the East Asian welfare regimes Confucian?

Earlier I stated that the debate over East Asian welfare regimes started out by suggesting that they were Confucian, but I concluded that this perspective had largely been given up by the scholarly community reflecting the criticism it had been met with (Abrahamson 2011). However, returning to the debate, it has proven longer lived or it has resurfaced to a large extent. This probably to some extent reflects China's 11th 5-year plan for 2006–2010 which focused on building a harmonious (socialist) society by, among other things, emphasizing the expansion of welfare policies (Fan 2006). Harmonious society is an obvious reference to Confucius and in a document explaining China's way to a universal welfare state the introduction directly and in some detail quotes Confucius' *Book of Rites* (China Development Research Foundation 2012). Following Solinger (2015, pp. 977–978) 'much have been made of the recent revival of Confucianism in the People's Republic of China (PRC), with its renewed promotion by the country's political leadership since the turn of the century. Among the chief teachings of that doctrine is the principle that the government has an unshakeable mission to "nourish the people" (yang min 养民).' In this vain, this section discusses not harmony but another of Confucius' central concepts namely *filial piety* with reference to East Asia and particularly China since it has become a very troubled issue as a consequence of the extremely low fertility rates that have developed in the region. Some authors are not in doubt, e.g. Leung (2014) stated, 'Hong Kong and four other Asian countries, namely Japan, Singapore, South Korea, and Taiwan, share certain common characteristics in terms of their welfare systems, which are based on Confucianism', and, as suggested, we could add China.

Izuhara and Ray (2013) compared three generations of families in Shanghai and Tokyo with an eye to housing, and they found that the family, far from, is an anachronistic institution. It is an active domain seeking to maximize benefits and opportunities for all its members. The traditional role of families appears to be rather robust and family support remains the dominant form of welfare provision.

In a paper by Chau and Yu (2013), the question of defamilization is directly related to the discussion of the East Asian welfare regime since they see it as a hallmark of modern welfare states and as an indication that society has moved away from the 'Confucian heritage' and they conclude 'there is almost a consensus that Confucianism in East Asia is no longer as influential as in the past' (Chau and Yu 2013, p. 357). Based on a cluster analysis of OECD and East Asian countries, they revealed a high level of diversity among the East Asian welfare regimes, and furthermore that some of them have a degree of defamilization similar to European countries, leading them to reject the assumption that East Asian countries cluster and are familistic. Interestingly, though, when the authors repeated the exercise (Yu *et al.* 2015, pp. 76–80), they spent full four pages discussing the application of the Confucian label to East Asian welfare regimes. Their overall conclusion is very cautious, 'In view of the above discussion, we should not take for granted the existence of the indispensable conditions for East Asian countries to form a Confucian welfare regime', indicating a revision of the aforementioned consensus that its influence is declining.

Another way of getting closer to whether Confucian norms prevail in the region is to investigate intergenerational relations as done by Lin and Yi (2013). Intergenerational co-residence varied between 48% in Taiwan and 24% in Korea; but, the living arrangement pattern was quite similar: more sons living with parents than daughters, which suggests that the four societies seem to maintain patriarchal norms. In addition, intergenerational contact was frequent in all four societies (Lin and Yi 2013, p. 304). They found among the four East Asian countries that 'the shared dominant patriarchal culture expresses itself by the continuing influence of filial norms on intergenerational relations between adult children and their parents. Sons tend to perform various filial duties much more than daughters' (Lin and Yi 2013, p. 312).

Phillips and Jung (2013) discuss familialism as the starting point for their qualitative research in Korea on social assistance since it is 'particularly relevant to East Asian welfare states, which have been characterized as sharing Confucian social norms and ethical values' (Phillips & Jung, 2013, p. 19). Thus, they maintain that ideas such as filial piety, individual self-help and family interdependence have been emphasized as social virtues in South Korea. Furthermore, they demonstrate that 'Confucian traditions have been institutionalized in social policies, and in this discussion they emerge as significant ideational and cultural factors that define current policy arrangements of the East Asian welfare states' (Phillips & Jung, 2013, pp. 19–20). It is so because in order to qualify for social assistance, National Basic Livelihood Security System, the applicant must not have a supporting family member. 'Justified by the tradition of Confucian familial piety the priority of family support is politically promoted and remains pervasive' (Phillips & Jung, 2013, p. 26).

Investigating filial piety with data for China, Taiwan and Hong Kong Yeh et al. found that 'filial piety ... remains potent among all three societies despite the diverse sociopolitical developments in each society... results confirm that filial piety has not been eroded by modernization and democratization' (2013, p. 292).

Proliferation and status of care policies in East Asia

In my paper from 2011, I suggested that East Asian welfare regimes to a large extent left care to the family. Care as such was not a right, but a culturally founded expectation. This perspective was a generalization based on literature published up to 2009 reflecting developments up to roughly 2005. Considering the situation about 10 years later may indeed call for a revision of the informality perspective considering the exponential speed of development in East Asia. This section tries to grasp the extent of family policy across the region by focusing on parental leave, childcare and care for the elderly country by country.

China

With the socialist revolution in China, gender equality was emphasized, but 'the transition from a centrally planned to a market economy that was launched in 1978 has led to a dramatic decline in publicly funded child care programs' (Du and Dong 2013, p. 132; see also, Hu 2014, p. 155) and maternity leave policies have not been enforced strongly. Hence, 'local governments and employers often circumvent these national policies. Most public sector employees have maternal leave benefits; however, in particular private enterprises, employers either disfavour hiring female workers or compromise women's maternity benefits' (Guo and Xiao 2013, p. 236). The overall conclusion regarding childcare in the literature is that 'childcare services remain underfunded and underdeveloped' (Yuan and Wang 2016, p. 25). Public services for the 0–2-year-olds have been dissolved and instead more than 61 million children are cared for by their grandparents; this is the so-called left behind children (Choi 2016, p. 131, Zhang et al. 2016, see also, 2014). There is no longer any public support for nurseries, so the price is preventive for many. On the other hand, Early Childhood Education Services has increased for the 3–5-year-olds and in 2010 the State council decided that they should be universal and in 2012 they had reached 62%, up from 28% in 1991 (Li et al. 2016, p. 427).

Similar development has happened with respect to elderly care. Chinese care for the elderly has traditionally been a family affair. The market has proven only to be an alternative solution for better off Chinese, which has led to the apparent paradoxical situation of enormous over capacity in the private for-profit nursing home sector at the same time as many Chines desperately need institutional care, but the capacity in the affordable public nursing homes is much too small to meet demands. Most cities apply the 90-7-3 formula meaning that they aim for 90% cared in own home, 7% in community care and 3% in institutions (Abrahamson, 2015). Several studies have shown the negative effect on women's labour market participation due to the care deficit (Chen et al. 2014, Du & Dong, 2013, Hare 2016), which is probably why the central authorities now advocate more public care; but the problem remains the resistance both from companies, local governments and not least prevailing gender roles and familistic orientations.

Japan

Regarding Japan, many observers associate the introduction of the Long Term Care Insurance (LTCI) in 2000 with an effort on behalf of the government to reduce cost of elderly care. The system took inspiration from the similar German programme; it is part of social insurance, which means that it is financed by workers' and employers' contributions and state funding, reflecting government policy to include all of society in financing. LTCI Subscribers 65+ can receive care services at a reduced price after their care needs have been assessed by the municipality (Abe 2010, p. 27). Yet, most care is still provided by family members, 'Spouses make up the largest number of main care providers (28 percent), followed by children (25.4 percent) and their spouses (18.1 percent). Professional care providers comprise only 9.9 percent;' and 'about 17 per cent of those who need care are in institutions, while the rest receive care while living at home' (Abe 2010, p. 17, 19). This reflects what Olivares-Tirado and Tamiya (2014) have termed the fourth phase of the LTCI plan (2009–2011) which introduced community-based services, including such initiatives as small-scale multifunctional care, night-time home-visit care service, group homes that are able to care for dementia patients and specially designated small-scale nursing homes for the elderly to continue their life in a community with which they are familiar.

There are three types of childcare in Japan, licensed and unlicensed day care centres and kindergartens. The latter is part of the educational system and provide for 3–5-year olds, while the former two provide for the youngest. The unlicensed centres tend to be in-house or firm based. The licensed centres tend to be municipal and they were attended by 31% of preschool children in Japan (Abe 2010, p. 30). So, all together, a fair to a large amount of children are cared for in some kind of institutional arrangement. Fees are heavily subsidized and are lower for low-income parents. Furthermore, parents receive financial support via child allowances which have been expanded significantly since 2000 and in 2008 they reached 90% of children under 12 (Abe 2010, p. 15). Given the above description, denying Japan the label of a welfare state would be absurd.

Korea

Like many other observers, Fleckenstein and Lee (2014) noticed that with the election of the first centre-left government (1998–2002), family policy was expanded, paid maternity leave was extended to 3 months; and a 12-month parental leave scheme was made available to all workers with children under 1 year of age; tax-based childcare benefits were expanded with the introduction of free childcare for 5 year-olds from low-income families. Furthermore, under the second centre-left government (2003–2007), family policy experienced what they call 'a remarkable expansion, indicating a challenge to the male breadwinner and liberal welfare trajectory' (Fleckenstein and Lee 2014, p. 620) indicated by a fourfold increase of the childcare budget between 2003 and 2006. This expansion of family policy was continued under consecutive Conservative governments and Lee and Fleckenstein explain it with reference to a combination of functional necessities of new risks *and* civil society groups as political drivers.

Through a similar comparative study of parental leave arrangements, Lee (2015) reaches a more pessimistic conclusion. She compared maternal, paternal and parental leave from a life – work balance, but she looked beyond policy formulations and found that 'opposite to what can be found in western nations leave legislation has been ineffective in South Korea since family leave laws were adopted as a means to achieve the ranks of a developed nation, with little consideration as to internal cultural values. Traditional influences of Confucianism, which support gender inequality have hindered implementation of family leave laws' (Lee 2015, p. 45).

This is also the starting point for Won (2016) in her study on working mothers in Korea. She stated that 'In Korea, existing studies have largely focused on "the appearance" of policy measures for work–family balance … [However], Policy rhetoric *per se* does not necessarily guarantee policy effectiveness'. She also identified a radical change in men's perception of women working from 12% agreeing to 54% agreeing, leading to a situation where 'Korean married men are much more likely to expect their wives to share the breadwinning burden; that is, society is moving toward a dual-earner reality' (Won 2016, p. 150); but this has not been accompanied by fathers being more involved in care work as demonstrated by a time-use study showing that men spent only 38 min on average on domestic care work per day, with 37 min for single-earner households and 39 min for dual-earner households (Won 2016, p. 151). She found that gender stereotypes contribute negatively to women's satisfaction of their work-life balance and that this is related to the persistence of Confucian values within Korean society, which considers mothers working as incompatible with the traditional role assigned to women.

Focusing on elderly care, Kim and Choi (2013) analysed the LTCI. They wanted to test whether Confucianism still remains strong in LTCI, and they concluded that despite elements of family care in the LTCI 'the current situation shows the consolidation of the Korean welfare state and increases the sense of welfare as a right. This could imply that the Korean welfare state is neither the developmental nor Confucian welfare state it used to be. It seems that developmentalism and Confucianism have been shifted from the centre of the Korean welfare state to the peripheral area ... Developmentalism seems to be quickly replaced by liberal principles' (2013, p. 883).

Taiwan

Chou *et al.* (2015, p. 95) began their paper by stating that 'different from some Western countries, care for frail older people in Taiwan remains a private responsibility and a family obligation, as the country belongs to the familistic East Asian welfare regime'. They sum up that there are four main models of long-term care (LTC) for older people in Taiwan, institutional care, community and home-based care, live-in migrant care and family care, and it is distributed thus: the majority of older people with care needs lived with family and were cared only by their family. The second largest group was those older people who were cared by migrant care workers, and the third group used institutional care. Only a very small proportion used community/home-based care services (Chou *et al.* 2015, p. 95; see also, Lin and Huang 2016). However, a LTCI is already in the legislative pipeline.

With respect to childcare, it has gradually been expanded and expenditure for children increased from 2% of total social benefits in 2000, to more than 7% in 2009. However, 'The demand for infant care is strong, and many infant centers are filled to capacity, and some of them have long waiting lists' (Chiu and Wei 2011). Parental leave was enacted in 2002, allowing both male and female employees to take up to 2 years of unpaid parental leave, shared between the partners. In 2009, parental leave benefits were implemented, offering 60% wage compensation for 6 months to each parent taking leave, thus allowing maximum paid leave of 1 year.

Still, according to Chang (2015), a very large minority of 45.5% believe that mothers who stay at home and care for their children is the best childcare arrangement. This social expectation is reflected in the reality that 95% of children under the age of 3 are cared for at home, and most of them are cared for by parents or unpaid relatives. Therefore, Chang (2015) investigated the determinants of household composition from the perspective of childcare arrangements. And she found that the presence of children under age 3 is still significantly associated with household composition, which supports the argument that people with young children are more likely to co-reside with elderly parents or extended kin.

In order to determine degrees of defamilization over time, An and Peng carried out a fuzzy-set analysis by constructing three indicators of labour- money and time defamilization, respectively, for 2000, 2005 and 2010. For Taiwan, the analysis showed no change, it stayed explicit familialism (An and Peng 2016, p. 14). They sum up thus, 'The degree of LDF [labor defamilization] and MDF [money defamilization] is lowest in Taiwan, suggesting that childcare services play a very minor role in encouraging women to be engaged in paid work' (An and Peng 2016, p. 16).

Hong Kong

Apart from important services such as healthcare and housing, Hong Kong provides very modest cover of social services. 88.9% of older people do not receive any services and 88.4% of children under the age of 3 are not placed in day nurseries, but it does provide financial support for older people to purchase personal care in private residential homes (Lai and Chui 2014, p. 268). Thus, unquestionably the family is considered the primary caregiver in Hong Kong. This is confirmed by Fung (2014) 'levels of financial support for personal social services has been strictly limited, with continual residualisation over recent decades'. Fung summed up thus, 'As a whole, the social groups receiving higher levels of public resources are mainly middle class rather than disadvantaged groups .... The government presumes that the family institution will shoulder the responsibility of caretaking for the young, the old, those with disabilities and the disadvantaged. Overall, the social policy features of the developmental state are clearly not alien to Hong Kong' (2014, p. 325).

Regarding day care, Leung (2014) considers Hong Confucian leading to an inadequate public delivery of services. She shows that there are programmes, but insufficiently available, with a chronic shortage and inaccessibility. The cost of childcare services is expensive for working-class families and private alternatives like child minders are too expensive. Leung concluded that childcare is perceived as the responsibility of the family, which in all reality means women, and not as a right of citizens.

Regarding care services for elderly, Cheng et al. (2013, p. 529) recorded that 'HK has a very imbalanced LTC system that depends heavily on residential care .... The institutionalization rate of older people is high, at 6.8 percent of people aged 65 years and older. Still, 28,000 older people are on the waiting list for residential care placement. To rebalance the LTC system, the government is implementing a new community-care voucher program, which is intended to lower the demand for residential care.' These authors consider the system untenable. 'The rate of poverty among older adults increased from 27.7 percent in 1991 to 38.7 percent in 2001, and then to 41.4 percent in 2011' (Lee and Chou 2015, p. 1). This testifies to the inability of familial support to bring about a decent retirement for 4 out of 10 older people in Hong Kong.

Singapore

Singapore provides paid parental leave for employees; married women are guaranteed 16 weeks in contrast to fathers' 1 week and unmarried mothers' 12 weeks. The short 1-week paternity leave, introduced in early 2013, is state funded. In contrast, unmarried women are entitled to leave but receive no public funding at all (Teo 2015b, p. 83).

Recently, day care facilities have been established and from 2009 to 2014, childcare centre places increased from 67.980 to 104.774, while infant care centre places increased from 2011 to 5.329 according to Teo (2016). This expansion of the formal childcare sector has happened in the past 5 years. (Teo 2016). Yet, a large part of childcare is still provided by grandparents.

Regarding care for the elderly it is also in the main considered a family responsibility since alternatives are limited and in short supply. According to Østbye et al., rehabilitation and day care centres have been established for older persons at the community level, and home care services provide a range of services including household chores, meal delivery, escort to clinics and hospitals and befriender services. 'However, the availability and accessibility of such home and community-based services remains limited and is a major concern for the elderly population and their families' (2013, p. 609).

As is the case in Taiwan and Hong Kong, families that can afford it employ foreign care workers to care for frail elderly. What is special about Singapore is that institutional care is also to a large extent provided by migrant care workers, 'The low prestige and wages alongside hard and dirty work associated with long-term eldercare have meant that it is being undertaken increasingly by female migrant workers in both types of spaces when family members and local workers are unable or reluctant to take on the labour. Foreign domestic workers providing eldercare are expected to dole out primarily physical care, while migrant healthcare workers are valorized for their skills *and* care attributes' (Huang et al. 2012, p. 210). Hence, Singapore is part of the increasing care chain and care drain. Furthermore, the current situation with 20% of the residents not being citizens (Straughan 2012) creates tensions based on racism and leaves the immigrant population with fewer rights than the ones enjoyed by those having citizenship.

Conclusion

The paper started out by asking whether East Asia is (still) subordinating social policies to economic development? And are they (still) dominated by familialism? The main part of the paper then discussed care policies in the region in order to challenge the assumption that it is characterized by care not being a state responsibility but a family affair, i.e. being informal. As to be expected within social science, the literature proposed contradictory answers to these questions.

Recent literature agrees that productivist and developmental are precise characterization of the three city-states of Macau, Hong Kong and Singapore. There is also a (near) agreement that Japan has moved or is moving away from this position towards the Conservative regime type. Considering Korea and Taiwan, the literature agrees that they have experienced rather similar developments, but there is disagreement as to whether they are stuck with being productivist and developmental, or whether the change from authoritarianism to democracy and the resulting social policy increases have moved them to the Liberal regime. Regarding China, there is agreement that changes have been significant and enormous, because of marketization and political reactions to its negative side effects. The two latest 5-year plans have committed China to create a universal welfare state, but the implementation leaves much room for improvement and a lot to be desired. Simultaneously, the Chinese Government has emphasized Confucian virtues and underlined the obligation to stay in touch with old parents.

Turning to the question of Confucianism, the literature consulted in this paper, it suggested the 'revenge of culture' or 'Confucianism strikes back' to be the most precise characterizations of the current situation prevailing in East Asia. Yes, societal conditions have changed – the region has modernized, and, yes social security and care policies have been expanded, but culture has proven to be stickier than what was expected some years ago. This has to a large extent escaped observations based in political science that has focused on democratization and the supposedly concomitant significant expansion of welfare policies. It is from sociology, and particularly feminist scholarship we have learned that the implemented policies to a large extent are based in a persistence of familial ideology and traditional gender roles, which de facto prevents the desired outcomes with respect to women's labour market participation and fertility. Thus, this conclusion is parallel to the one reached by the authors in Sung and Pascall (2014) where Confucianism is seen as the root cause of varied situations of gender inequality.

Undoubtedly, there has been a significant development of social care services across East Asia. Disagreements surface when judging whether these changes and developments break with original or previous modes, or whether path dependency prevails. The latter proposition is based on either viewing changes as merely lip service, or not breaking with traditional views on gender and family inherited from Confucianism, while the former adds up changes particularly of a universal kind leading to a break with the past and entering one of the Western paths. All things considered, I conclude that Japan has moved to the Conservative regime, while Macau, Hong Kong and Singapore have remained within the productivist/developmental regime since the introduction and expansion of care policies have been rather limited and inconsequential; the levels of inequality and poverty are incompatible with a European style welfare state. As regards China it remains to be seen if the official commitment to a universal welfare regime type is going to be realized in the foreseeable future, but the current level of inequality is not encouraging. The most difficult cases to judge are those of Korea and Taiwan, and this is also where the literature is most in disagreement. For very good reasons, Powell and Kim's paper on Korea was entitled 'The "Chameleon" Korean Welfare Regime' indicating that it constantly changes appearance depending on the approach. Despite the significant expansion of care policies, I side with the feminists pointing out that the policies to a large extent are based on and implemented in a familial ideology that in reality confirms traditional roles rather than liberating women concluding that Korea may be post-developmental and on the move towards a liberal regime, but is still confined within a Confucian one together with Taiwan.

To the question as to whether the whole region can be characterized by one overarching concept, the papers considered here overwhelmingly point to the persistence of filial piety, yet more in the reciprocal than in the authoritarian sense, as the guiding principle for solidarity both on the individual and the state level, suggesting that the label Confucian welfare regime remains very adequate.

Disclosure statement

No potential conflict of interest was reported by the author.

References

Abe, A.K. 2010. *The changing shape of the care diamond, the case of child and elderly care in Japan.* Gender and Development Programme No 9. Geneva: UNRISD.

Abrahamson, P., 1999. The welfare modelling business. *Social Policy & Administration*, 33 (4), 394–415. doi:10.1111/spol.1999.33.issue-4

Abrahamson, P. 2011. The welfare modelling business revisited: the case of East Asian welfare regimes. Gyu-jin Hwang (ed.) New Welfare States in East Asia: Global Challenges and Restructuring. Cheltenham: Edward Elgar Publishing Ltd., pp. 15–34.

Abrahamson, P. 2015. Gender and welfare regimes revised: connecting chinese and danish perspectives. *Women, Gender & Research*, 2015 (1), 67–79.

Ahn, S.-H. and Lee, S.-Y.S., 2012. Explaining Korean welfare state development with new Empirical data and methods'. *Asian Social Work and Policy Review*, 6, 67–85. doi:10.1111/j.1753-1411.2012.00063.x

An, M.Y. and Peng, I., 2016. Diverging paths? A comparative look at childcare policies in Japan, South Korea and Taiwan. *Social Policy & Administration*, 50 (5), 540–558. doi:10.1111/spol.2016.50.issue-5

Chang, Y.-H., 2015. Childcare needs and household composition: is household extension a way of seeking childcare support? *Chinese Sociological Review*, 47 (4), 343–366. doi:10.1080/21620555.2015.1062345

Chau, R.C.M. and Yu, S.W.K., 2013. Defamilisation of twenty-two countries its implications for the study of East Asian welfare regime. *Social Policy & Society*, 12 (3), 355–367. doi:10.1017/S1474746412000577

Chen, J., Shao, X., Murtaza, G., and Zhao, Z., 2014. Factors that influence female labor force supply in China. *Economic Modelling*, 37 (4), 485-491.

Cheng, S.-T., et al., 2013. Hong Kong: embracing a fast aging society with limited welfare. *The Gerontologist*, 53 (4), 527–533. doi:10.1093/geront/gnt017

China Development Research Foundation, 2012. *Constructing a social welfare system for all in China.* London: Routledge.

Chiu, C.-P. and Wei, S., 2011. Child care friendly policies and integration of ECEC in Taiwan. *International Journal of Child Care and Education Policy*, 5 (2), 1–19. doi:10.1007/2288-6729-5-2-1

Choi, S.Y.P., 2016. Children and migration in China. *Asian Population Studies*, 12 (2), 131–134. doi:10.1080/17441730.2016.1150637

Choi, Y.J., 2012. End of the era of productivist welfare capitalism? Diverging welfare regimes in East Asia. *Asian Journal of Social Science*, 40 (3), 275–294. doi:10.1163/156853112X650827

Chou, Y.-C., Kröger, T., and Pu, C.-Y., 2015. Models of long-term care use among older people with disabilities in Taiwan: institutional care, community care, live-in migrant care and family care. *European Journal of Ageing*, 12 (2), 95–104. doi:10.1007/s10433-014-0322-z

Du, F., and Dong, X.-Y., 2013. Women's employment and child care choices in urban china during the economic transition. *Economic Development and Cultural Change*, 62 (1), 131-155. doi:10.1086/671714

Du, F. and Dong, X.-Y., 2013. Women's employment and child care choices in urban China during the economic transition. *Economic Development and Cultural Change*, 62 (1), 131–155. doi:10.1086/671714

Fan, C., 2006. China's eleventh five-year plan (2006–2010), from 'getting rich first' to 'common prosperity.'. *Eurasian Geography and Economics*, 47 (6), 708–723. doi:10.2747/1538-7216.47.6.708

Fleckenstein, T. and Lee, S.C., 2014. The politics of postindustrial social policy, family policy reforms in Britain, Germany, South Korea, and Sweden. *Comparative Political Studies*, 47 (4), 601–630. doi:10.1177/0010414012451564

Fung, K.K., 2014. Financial crisis and the developmental states: a case study of Hong Kong. *International Journal of Social Welfare*, 23, 321–332. doi:10.1111/ijsw.2014.23.issue-3

Guo, J. and Xiao, S., 2013. Through the gender lens: a comparison of family policy in Sweden and China. *China Journal of Social Work*, 6 (3), 228–243. doi:10.1080/17525098.2013.840663

Hare, D., 2016. What accounts for the decline in labor force participation among married women in urban China, 1991–2011? *China Economic Review*, 38 (2), 251–266. doi:10.1016/j.chieco.2016.01.004

Holiday, I., 2000. Productivist welfare capitalism, social policy in East Asia. *Political Studies*, 48, 706–723. doi:10.1111/1467-9248.00279

Hu, X., 2014. Childcare policy reform and women's labour force participation in China. *In*: Y. Atasoy, ed. *Global economic crisis and the politics of diversity*. London: Palgrave MacMillan, 155–177.

Huang, S., Yeoh, B.S.A., and Toyota, M., 2012. Caring for the elderly, the embodied labour of migrant care workers in Singapore. *Global Networks*, 12 (2), 195–215. doi:10.1111/j.1471-0374.2012.00347.x

Hwang, G.-J., 2012. Explaining welfare state adaptation in East Asia, the cases of Japan, Korea and Taiwan. *Asian Journal of Social Science*, 40 (2), 174–202. doi:10.1163/156853112X640134

Izuhara, M. and Ray, F., 2013. Active families,' familization, housing and welfare across generations in East Asia. *Social Policy & Administration*, 47 (5), 520–541. doi:10.1111/spol.12002

Jones, C., 1990. Hong Kong, Singapore, South Korea and Taiwan: oiconomic welfare states. *Government & Opposition*, 25 (4), 447–462. doi:10.1111/j.1477-7053.1990.tb00396.x

Jones, C., 1993. 'The Pacific challenge: Confucian welfare states. *In*: C. Jones, ed. *New perspectives on the welfare state in Europe*. London: Routledge, 198–217.

Kim, J.W. and Choi, Y.J., 2013. 'Farewell to old legacies? The introduction of long-term care insurance in South Korea. *Ageing and Society*, 33, 871–887. doi:10.1017/S0144686X12000335

Kim, W.S. and Shi, S.-J., 2013. Emergence of new welfare states in East Asia? domestic social changes and the impact of 'welfare internationalism' in South Korea and Taiwan (1945–2012). *International Journal of Social Quality*, 3 (2), 106–124.

Kwon, H.-J., 2005. An overview of the study, the developmental welfare state and policy reforms in East Asia. *In*: H.-J. Kwon, ed. *Transforming the developmental welfare state in East Asia*. New York: Palgrave Macmillan, 1–23.

Lai, D.W.L. and Chui, E.W.T., 2014. A tale of two cities, a comparative study on the welfare regimes of Hong Kong and Macao. *Social Policy and Society*, 13 (2), 263–274. doi:10.1017/S1474746413000614

Lee, M., 2015. Legislative initiative for work-family reconciliation in South Korea, A comparative analysis of the South Korean, American, French, and German family leave policies'. *Asian American Law Journal*, 22, 45–103.

Lee, S.-Y. and Chou, K.-L., 2015. Trends in elderly poverty in Hong Kong, A decomposition analysis. *Social Indicators Research*, 129 (2), 551–564.

Leung, L.C., 2014. Gender mainstreaming childcare policy, barriers in a confucian welfare society. *Journal of International and Comparative Social Policy*, 30 (1), 41–52. doi:10.1080/21699763.2014.886611

Li, K., et al., 2016. Early childhood education quality and child outcomes in China: evidence from Zhejiang Province. *Early Childhood Research Quarterly*, 36, 427–438. doi:10.1016/j.ecresq.2016.01.009

Lin, J. and Yi, C.C., 2013. A comparative analysis of intergenerational relations in East Asia. *International Sociology*, 28 (3), 297–315. doi:10.1177/0268580913485261

Lin, K. and Wong, C.K., 2013. Social policy and social order in East Asia, an evolutionary view. *Asia Pacific Journal of Social Work and Development*, 23 (4), 270–284. doi:10.1080/02185385.2013.778785

Lin, Y.Y. and Huang, C.-S., 2016. Aging in Taiwan, building a society for active aging and aging in place. *The Gerontologist*, 56 (2), 176–183. doi:10.1093/geront/gnv107

Mok, J., 2013. After the regional and global financial crisis, social development challenges and social policy responses in Hong Kong and Macau. *In*: M. Izuhara, ed. *Handbook on East Asian social policy*. Cheltenham: Edward Elgar.

Olivares-Tirado, P. and Tamiya, N., 2014. *Trends and factors in Japan's long-term care insurance system, Japan's 10-year experience*. Heidelberg: Springer.

Østbye, T., et al., 2013. Does support from foreign domestic workers decrease the negative impact of informal caregiving? Results from Singapore survey on informal caregiving. *The Journals of Gerontology Series B: Psychological Sciences and Social Sciences*, 68 (4), 609–621. doi:10.1093/geronb/gbt042

Phillips, R. and Jung, Y.M., 2013. The clash between social policy and traditional values: Unmet welfare needs sustained by the culture of familism in South Korea. *Asian Social Work and Policy Review*, 7 (1), 18–27. doi:10.1111/aswp.12004

Solinger, D.J., 2015. Three welfare models and current Chinese social assistance: Confucian justifications, variable applications. *The Journal of Asian Studies*, 74 (4), 977–999. doi:10.1017/S0021911815001126

Straughan, P.T., 2012. *Delayed marriages and ultra-low fertility, the confounding challenges to social stability*. Singapore: National University of Singapore.

Sung, S. and Pascall, G., eds., 2014. *Gender and welfare states in East Asia: Confucianism or gender equality*. London: Palgrave/MacMillan.

Teo, Y., 2015a. Interrogating the limits of welfare reforms in Singapore. *Development and Change*, 46 (1), 95–120. doi:10.1111/dech.2015.46.issue-1

Teo, Y., 2015b. Differentiated deservedness: governance through familialist social policies in Singapore. *Trans: Trans -Regional and -National Studies of Southeast Asia*, 3 (1), 73–93. doi:10.1017/trn.2014.16

Teo, Y., 2016. Not everyone has 'maids', class differentials in the elusive quest for work-life balance. *Gender, Place & Culture*, 23. doi:10.1080/0966369X.2015.1136810

Won, S.-Y., 2016. State policy? traditional gender stereotypes? relative contributions of factors affecting positive work–family interface for working mothers in Korea. *Gender, Work & Organization*, 23 (2), 147–164. doi:10.1111/gwao.v23.2

Yang, -J.-J., 2013. Parochial welfare politics and the small welfare state in South Korea. *Comparative Politics*, 45 (4), 457–475.

Yeh, K.-H, Yi, C.-C, Tsao, W.-C, and Wan, P.-S, 2013. Filial piety in contemporary chinese societies: a comparative study of Taiwan, Hong Kong, and China. *International Sociology*, 28 (3), 277-296. doi:10.1177/0268580913484345

Yu, S., Chau, C.M., and Lee, K.M., 2015. Using defamilisation typologies to study the Confucian welfare regime. *Journal of International and Comparative Social Policy*, 31 (1), 74–93. doi:10.1080/21699763.2014.992457

Yuan, P. and Wang, L., 2016. Migrant workers: China boom leaves children behind. *Nature*, 529, 25. doi:10.1038/529025a

Zhang, N., et al., 2016. Parental migration, intergenerational obligations and the paradox for left-behind boys in rural China. *Asian Population Studies*, 12 (1), 68–87. doi:10.1080/17441730.2015.1128230

Zhang, Z., Gu, D., and Luo, Y., 2014. Coresidence with elderly parents in contemporary China: the role of filial piety, reciprocity, socioeconomic resources, and parental needs. *Journal of Cross-Cultural Gerontology*, 29, 259–276. doi:10.1007/s10823-014-9239-4

RESEARCH ARTICLE

East Asia in transition: re-examining the East Asian welfare model using fuzzy sets

Nan Yang

ABSTRACT
East Asia's economic and social structures came under pressure in the aftermath of the Asian financial crisis in 1997 and the productivist welfare capitalism (PWC) thesis faced a fundamental challenge. This paper explores the veracity of the PWC thesis by exploring six social policy fields, including education, health care services, family, old-age pensions, housing and protective labour market policy, in China, Hong Kong, Japan, South Korea, Singapore and Taiwan using fuzzy-set ideal type analysis (FsITA). The findings suggest that it is inaccurate to talk about one single, homogeneous welfare model in East Asia. Despite persistent similarities in regard to their cultural foundations, cases in Greater China and East Asia have distinctive social policy development trajectories often combining 'productive' and 'protective' policies in unique ways.

Introduction

Since publication of Esping-Andersen's (1990) *The Three Worlds of Welfare Capitalism*, there have been questions whether East Asian states could sensibly be categorized into his welfare regime typology (see e.g. Esping-Andersen 1997, Holliday 2000, 2005, Gough 2001) and fierce debates regarding the existence of a distinct homogenous East Asian welfare model (Goodman *et al.* 1997, Kwon 2005, Aspalter 2006). While some scholars rejected this idea (Mishra 1995, Goodman *et al.* 1998, Hudson and Kühner 2012), others agreed that East Asian states featured important similarities in their welfare systems giving credence to the notion of an East Asian productivist welfare capitalism with its predominant focus on accelerating economic growth (Goodman and Peng 1996, Holliday 2000, 2005, Holliday and Wilding 2003).

However, cases across Greater China and East Asia have reformed their welfare systems in response to the 1997 Asian financial crisis. Holliday (2005, p. 147) recognized that after the financial crisis, the leading East Asian economies 'reveal[ed] their true social policy colours', but posited that the productivist classification remains 'plausible and useful'. Similarly, Kwon (2005, p. 494) noted that while the welfare system in Korea and Taiwan China (hereafter Taiwan) became more inclusive, the goals of its social policies have remained unchanged and are still used primarily for economic growth.

Aspalter (2011, p. 741) maintained his earlier view indicating that the level of direct redistribution remains low in East Asia and that social policy still remained the 'key ingredient to stable and continuous economic growth'. In contrast, writing about Republic of Korea (hereafter Korea), Kuhnle (2004, p. 61) argued that the Korean welfare system has developed policy structures that have 'more in common with the "Nordic" or Scandinavian, "social-democratic" welfare regime than any of the other European and Western types'.

Given the persistent ambiguity within the existing literature, this paper aims to revisit two crucial questions: first, is there a homogeneous welfare model in East Asia? And second, can this model still be characterized as 'productive'? In order to answer these questions, this paper focuses on six cases in Greater China and East Asia, namely China Mainland (hereafter China), Hong Kong, Special Administrative Region (SAR) of China (hereafter Hong Kong), Japan, Korea, Singapore and Taiwan. It explores six key policy fields in 2010, including education, healthcare services, family, old age pensions, housing and protective labour market policy using fuzzy-set ideal type analysis (FsITA) to overcome some of the methodological challenges that have plagued comparative welfare research (see e.g. Kim 2008 for a discussion). Due to a lack of hard quantitative data, the majority of studies have been carried out by indigenous scholars and provided in-depth descriptive accounts of individual cases (see e.g. Ku 1997, Takahashi 1997, Tang 1998). There are, of course, some cross-national studies (see e.g. Ramesh 2004, Aspalter 2005, 2006, Kwon; 2005, Walker and Wong 2005, Lee and Ku 2007), but the majority of these merely offered comparisons between one or two cases on one or two specific policy areas.

This paper shows that FsITA can overcome some of these data availability issues as it allows qualitative concepts to be compared quantitatively. This is because FsITA regards social phenomena as set relations by working with membership scores of cases in sets. The sets are understood as 'distinct and differing configurations of multiple, conceptually rooted, dimensions' (Hudson and Kühner 2010, p. 169), which reflect theoretical concepts and analytical constructs (Kvist 2007, Quaranta 2013a). FsITA also reflects the real extent of diversity between cases as particularly 'strong' or 'weak' features in one policy field will not bias its overall final results.

The paper is structured as follows. First, it will develop a new model for East Asian welfare policy including six key areas of social policymaking. Second, it will present an empirical application of this model by illustrating the FsITA calibration procedure for education policy in Greater China and East Asia, before – third – discussing all findings and their theoretical implications. The final section will conclude.

Conceptualizing the East Asian welfare model

In order to examine the East Asian welfare model, we first need to build a conceptual framework to enable systematic comparisons. For Holliday, for instance, there are two central arguments that are distinctive for productivist states: they follow a growth-oriented development strategy and all aspects of state policy including social policy are designed to achieve this goal (Holliday 2000, p. 709). Social policy in productive welfare states merely serves economic/industrial policy goals, which is a key difference between East Asian productivist welfare capitalism and traditional welfare states (Holliday 2005). Holliday (2005, 148) further argued that productivist social policy does not necessarily mean minimizing social protection: in a productivist state, social policy has some clear tasks 'led by education, but also taking in all other sectors'. Similarly, Wilding (2008, p. 22) summarized the role of productivist social policy as 'securing a ready supply of appropriately qualified personnel to service the economy, securing political and social stability, ensuring the smooth operation of the labour market and so on'. Put even more succinctly, Gough (2004, p. 190) stated that the key feature of productivist social policy is its emphasis on social investment rather than on social protection.

This latter point of view has been widely accepted and cited not only by East Asian welfare scholars. Most prevalent studies into East Asian welfare regimes have focused on distinguishing and weighting two dimensions of social policymaking: productive and protective welfare (see e.g. Holliday 2000, Rudra 2007, Hudson and Kühner 2012). Drawing on these discussions, three policy areas are chosen in this paper to measure the degree of productivism in East Asia, namely education, health care and family policy.

Education (E) has always been regarded as an important tool for promoting economic growth in the region as heavy investment in human capital is a key characteristic of a productivist welfare regime. Education has rarely been absent from research studies into welfare systems in East Asian states. It is also one of the fundamental policy fields of the PWC thesis (see discussion above). *Health care (H)* was proposed by William Beveridge in the famous Beveridge Report as one of the five most important services of a welfare state. Health care is also a key element of the PWC theory. However, in terms of classifying its welfare dimension, health service is an ambiguous policy field. Scholars have either regarded health care as a tool to secure a healthy labour force and increase the productivity of the labour force or pointed to the fact that a lack of health care has significant effects on public health, poverty, income generation, labour market productivity, economic growth and development (ILO 2016). In this paper, 'easy' and 'cheap' access to health care is regarded as a productive factor. *Family policies (F)* also serve both productive and protective objectives. On the protective side, working family support can ensure the health and well-being of children and mothers (Carneiro *et al.* 2011, Thévenon and Solaz 2013) and reduce poverty. Yet, from a productive angle, it can also support those with caring responsibilities to reconcile family obligations and working careers and lead to higher (female) employment in particular (Cerise *et al.* 2013). For instance, Jaumotte (2003) analysed six policy areas which might influence the female labour participation rate, including family taxation, childcare subsidies and child benefits, parental leave, flexibility of working time arrangements, anti-discrimination laws and other indirect policies, and showed that the supply of affordable childcare and the provision of parental leave have a significant effect on boosting female participation everything else being equal. Especially, maternity leave[1] as an indispensable element of comprehensive work-family policies plays an important role in preserving the mother's and her newborn's health (Addati *et al.* 2014) and incentivizing women's employment in the labour market (Baker and Milligan 2008, Feng and Han 2010, Misra *et al.* 2011, Cerise *et al.* 2013, Thévenon and Solaz 2013).

On the protective side, this paper mainly follows Esping-Andersen (1990) and the ensuing 'welfare modelling business'. It selects three policy areas, namely old-age income protection, housing policy and passive labour market policy. *Old-age income protection (I)* is particularly important for research on East Asia due to significant demographic changes in the region. The aging problem is occurring much more rapidly in the region compared with Organisation for Economic Co-operation and Development (OECD) countries (Fu and Hughes 2009). *Housing (P)* has often been omitted in comparative welfare research (see e.g. Wilensky 1975, Esping-Andersen 1990), but most scholars have accepted that it is an important pillar of any welfare state (Kemeny 2001). Hill (1996) suggested that housing policy is a crucial tool to eliminate inequality and poverty as it accounts for a very large part of household needs. Similarly, Brhane *et al.* (2014, p.27) argued that public rental housing is 'the most direct government investment in expanding the overall supply of low-cost housing' and a basic safety net for families with a per capita income below the poverty line. Finally, for Hoekstra (2003, p. 60), housing de-commodification can be defined as 'the extent to which households can provide their own housing, independent of the income they acquire on the labour market'. *Passive labour market policy (U)* is also often explored in comparative welfare studies in East Asia (see e.g. Lee and Ku 2007; Hudson and Kühner 2012). Unemployment benefits protect the income of individuals against the risk of job loss resulting in a period of job search. It thus plays an important role in helping individuals to maintain their standard of living when formal employment is lost (Packard and Nguyen 2014).

In using the above policy fields, FsITA employs set-theoretic methods to identify ideal types. Three principles of the set-theoretic theory are essential for combining sets – the logical AND, logical OR and logical NOT (Ragin 2000). The logical 'AND' is used in order to denote a combination of sets. A symbol '*' is used to denote this operation. It is also called the minimum rule as the minimum value of the combined sets is used. The logical OR describes a disjunction between sets and is formally denoted as '+'. The fuzzy-set score of logical OR is the maximum value of the two sets. The third principle is the rule of negation, which is also called logical NOT. The calculation of the logical NOT is a subtraction of the case's membership from 1. All possible combinations of these sets constitute the so-called multidimensional property or vector space (Kvist 1999). Here, the three 'productive' and the three 'protective' policy fields lead to $2^6 = 64$ ideal types, which can be clustered into four aggregated models: productive welfare, protective welfare, balanced welfare and underdeveloped welfare. Total 15 sub-models were identified under these aggregated models. Figure 1 illustrates the property space of the East Asian welfare models with detailed interpretations displayed in Table 1.

The productive welfare model denotes that a case has significant productive features, and that its protective features are comparatively weak. In other words, within this model 'productivism' weighs much heavier than 'protectivism'. Three sub-models are specified under the productive welfare model. The ultimate productive and weak productive welfare models are two purely productive welfare models, both with strong productive features and non-membership of protective dimensions. The difference between the two is that the ultimate type has membership of all productive dimensions while the moderate type only has membership to two of the three productive characteristics. Unlike the other two types, the hybrid productive model not only has all three productive features, but also has one protective characteristic. The protective welfare model and its three sub-models follow the same logic of the above classifications, but with emphasis on the 'protective' rather than 'productive' policy area. For example, the ultimate protective welfare type is similar to the ultimate productive

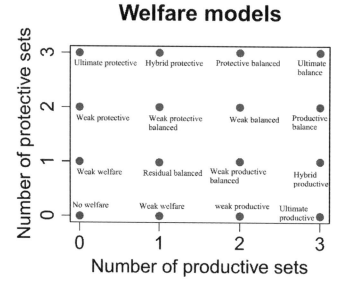

Figure 1. Welfare models.

welfare type, which has memberships of all protective sets and no membership of productive sets.

The balanced welfare model stands between the productive model and the protective model, with membership of both the productive and the protective dimensions. Here, seven sub-models were identified. The ultimate balanced model is the extreme version of the balanced model with memberships of all the six welfare dimensions. The weak balanced model is a downgraded version of the ultimate model with membership of two productive sets and two protective sets. Following the same logic, the residual balanced model has membership of one productive set and one protective set. Unlike the three balanced models discussed above, both the productive balanced and the weak productive balanced models have more memberships of productive sets than of protective sets: the productive balanced model has three productive sets and two protective sets, whereas the weak productive balanced model has two productive sets and one protective set. The protective balanced and the weak protective balanced models follow the same logic. Finally, the underdeveloped welfare model denotes that a country's welfare system is underdeveloped, with membership to only one welfare dimension.

Re-examining the East Asian welfare using fuzzy sets

Before the classification of cases across Greater China and East Asia can be tested empirically, calibration is crucially important to determine the membership of cases to sets. In FsITA, three basic qualitative breakpoints, '1', '0.5' and '0', refer to whether a case is 'fully in', 'neither in nor out' or 'fully out' of a set, respectively. For instance, if a case scores '1' in education set, it means this case has comparatively 'strong' education service. Scholars need to decide the benchmark of a strong education service according

Table 1. East Asian welfare model.

Welfare models	Welfare sub-models	Characteristics	Models
Productive welfare models	Ultimate productive model	Membership of the education service set (E), health service set (H), and family policy set (F) only	EHFipl
	Weak productive model	Membership of two productive sets, and non-membership of all the protective sets	EHFipl EhFipl eHFipl
	Hybrid productive	Membership of all the productive sets and one protective set.	EHFIpl EHFiPl EHFipL
Protective welfare models	Ultimate protective model	Membership of the old-age income protection set (I), housing policy set(P) and passive labour market policy set(L) only	ehfIPL
	Weak protective model	Membership of two protective sets, and non-membership of all the productive sets	ehfIpL ehfiPL ehflPl
	Hybrid protective	Membership of all the protective sets and one productive set.	EhfIPL eHfIPL ehFIPL
Balanced models	Ultimate balanced model	Membership of all the welfare sets	EHFIPL
	Weak balanced model	Membership of two productive sets and two protective sets.	EHfIPl EHFIpL EHFiPL eHFIpL eHFiPL eHFIPl EhFIPl EhFIpL EhFiPL
	Productive balanced model	Membership of all productive sets and two protective sets.	EHFIPl EHFIpL EHFiPL
	Weak productive balanced model	Membership of two productive sets and one protective set.	EHfiPl EHfIpl EHfipL eHFiPl eHFIpl eHFipL EhFiPL EhFIpl EhFipL
	Protective balanced model	Membership of all protective sets and two productive sets.	EHfIPL EhFIPL eHFIPL
	Weak protective balanced model	Membership of two protective sets and one productive set.	IPIEhf IPIeHf IPlehF IpLEhf IpLeHf IpLehF iPLEhf iPLeHf iPLehF
	Residual balanced welfare	Membership of one productive set and one protective set only	Ehflpl EhfiPl EhfipL eHflpl eHfiPl eHfipL ehFlpl ehFiPl ehFipL
Underdeveloped welfare	No welfare	Non-membership of all the sets	ehfipl
	Weak welfare	Membership of one set only	Ehfipl eHfipl ehFipl ehfIpl ehfiPl ehfipL

to theoretical and substantive knowledge (Ragin 2000). Because in most cases, there is no clear guidebook for what is a 'strong' or 'weak' welfare service, this benchmarking exercise is not always straightforward or easy. Three main strategies are used in this paper to achieve robust calibration of sets: a comparison of raw indicator scores across the region and the world; conventions of international organizations and case knowledge. Due to the word limit of this article, only 'education service' is discussed as an example to illustrate the process of calibration. The full details of the breakpoints for all policy areas are available from the author upon request. Table 2 shows the summary of empirical indicators and their fuzzy interval scores of the six policy fields.[2]

An education service can be expressed in fuzzy set terms as the ideal typical location – SPENDING * GENEROUS*ACCESSBILITY – or in plain English, a better education service is characterized by high public spending on education, a generous mandatory education service and easy access to higher education. The emphasis on education across Greater China and East Asia is reflected in high public SPENDING (S) (Table 3). The fully in point of the spending set was set at 20%, the fully out point at 10% and the crossover point at 15%. These cut-off points are mainly based on Hudson and Kühner's (2009) argument that education is one of the five core pillars of the welfare state (education, health service, housing, social security and employment). Theoretically, all five aspects should be given equal emphasis, and a 20% share of each aspect was set as the middle point in their work. However, during the last two decades, the education spending of the OECD average has never reached 20%. So in this paper, 20% was set as the fully in point, with 10% as the fully out point. In terms of the GENEROSITY (G) of an education service, the cases that are fully in the set have free compulsory pre-university education, including kindergarten, primary and secondary education. Countries with 8-year free compulsory primary education were set as neither in nor out of the set. The cases that are fully out of the set have no free compulsory education service. 'Free education' is narrowly defined as 'education without the need to pay any tuition fees'. In 2010, among the six cases, China, Japan, Korea and Taiwan all have 9-year free compulsory education. Singapore has 6-year free compulsory education, but achieved universal lower secondary education in 1970 through heavily subsidizing secondary education. Hong Kong is the only[3] case in this study that has 12-year free education.

Access to higher education is essential for both national development and individual advancement (Altbach 2006). The ACCESSIBILITY (A) of tertiary education for students in financial difficulties was therefore adopted as a separate measure in this paper. Tuition fees, the availability of student loans and access to financial aid were considered for scoring. Similar to the set G, as there was no comparable hard data, which could be used, the qualitative method of calibration was adopted for this set. China's average tuition fee has reached around 6000 Yuan (nearly £600 sterling) in 2009. Although much lower than in OECD countries and in the other five East Asian cases, considering the average income, tuition fees at this level are still difficult to afford for many Chinese families. According to China's social security system development report (Wang 2012), supporting one student to complete tertiary education in China required 4.2 years' net income of an urban worker or 13.6 years' net income of a peasant. Tuition fees increased 25 times between 1989 and 2009. Meanwhile, China has numerous tuition subsidies, including student loans, grants, scholarships, work-study funds and tuition-cost waiving, but all of these are strictly needs- or merit-based and meaning only a limited proportion of students can access financial aid.

Both Japan and Korea have been classified by the OECD into the group with high tuition fees and less-developed student support systems (OECD 2012). Most students in these two countries are charged high tuition fees compared with other OECD countries. In addition, a comparatively low level of public expenditures on tertiary education

Table 2. Empirical indicators and fuzzy set interval scores.

Area	Empirical indicator	Fully in the set 1.00	Almost in the set 0.83–0.99	Fairly in the set 0.67–0.82	More or less in the set 0.51–0.66	Neither in nor out of the set 0.5	Fairly out of the set 0.33–0.49	Mostly out of the set 0.17–0.32	Almost out of the set 0.01–0.16	Fully out of the set 0.00
Education	*Spending* measured by ratio of public education expenditure in total public expenditure (%)	>20				15				<10
	Generosity measured by the duration and cost of compulsory education	12-year free education	-	9-year free education	-	8-year free education		6-year free education		No free education
	Accessibility measured by the difficulty for affordability of higher education	Easy to afford/unselective student loan, Various financial aids available; easy for students with financial difficulties access to tertiary education	-	-		Moderate/ Fairly easy for students with financial difficulties access to tertiary education				Difficult to afford/Very strict selective financial aids; hard for students with financial difficulties access to tertiary education
Health	*Spending* measured by the proportion of public health expenditure in total public expenditure (%)	>14				10				<6.9
	Universality measured by the coverage of public health service (%)	>80				50				<20
	Affordability measured by the percentage of private expenditure (% of total health expenditure)	<31				35				>52
Family policy	*Generosity* measured by net replacement rate of maternity leave (%)	>75				66				<20
	Duration	>24				18				<14
	Coverage measured by the proportion of insured employees in the total employees (%)	100				50				0

(Continued)

Table 2. (Continued).

Area		Empirical indicator	Fully in the set 1.00	Almost in the set 0.83–0.99	Fairly in the set 0.67–0.82	More or less in the set 0.51–0.66	Neither in nor out of the set 0.5	Fairly out of the set 0.33–0.49	Mostly out of the set 0.17–0.32	Almost out of the set 0.01–0.16	Fully out of the set 0.00
Old age income protection	*Pillar zero pension*	Pension programmes	With pillar zero pension								No pillar zero pension
	Mandatory pension	Generosity measured by average net replacement rate (%)	>75 High				50 Medium				<20 Low
		Universality of old-age pension (%)	Universal 83				Selective 50				Residual <10
Housing	*Public rental policy*		With well-developed public rental housing				With public rental housing but under development				Without any public rental policy
Passive labour market policy		Generosity measured by monthly payment compared with minimum wage (%)	>75				50				<20
		Coverage (%)	73				50				<10
		Duration shows the total weeks paid	14.8				13				0

Table 3. Public education expenditures of six East Asian cases (as % of total government expenditure) in 2010.

Cases	Public education expenditure (as% of total government expenditure)
China	13.96
Hong Kong	18.94
Japan	8.73
Korea	15.00
Singapore	21.02
Taiwan	20.13

Source: ADB (2012), Ministry of Education Taiwan (2013)

indicates that only a small proportion of students benefit from public loans. In Japan, a new means-tested student loan system was introduced in 2004 under the Independent Administrative Institution Japan Student Services Organisation (JASSO) (JASSO 2014). To be able to apply, a student must meet both income-based and merit-based criteria. Only 27% of tertiary students were participating in the two lending programmes in 2008 (Newby et al. 2009), and this figure increased to 33% in 2010 (OECD 2012). In Korea, the support system is more comprehensive. Besides selection-based student loans, Korea also introduced a new income-dependent loan programme from 2010 (referred to as the Study-Now-Pay-Later programme) (Lee 2010). Students are required to pay back the loan within 25 years of attaining employment. This type of student loan is quite similar to the student loans in Western countries. The Korean government has stated that this programme might enable about half of university students to continue studying (The Korea Times 2009).

The tuition fees in Hong Kong have remained at HK$42,100 from 1997 until the present. The Hong Kong government reviews tuition fee levels annually and the Hong Kong government's education policy is to ensure that 'no qualified students are deprived of education through lack of means' (University Grants Committee 2010, p. 33). The Tertiary Student Finance Scheme (TSFS) for publicly funded programmes provides means-tested financial assistance to full-time students in the form of a grant and/or loan. The levels of grants and loans are calculated on the basis of 'Adjusted Family Income' (AFI). In addition, from the late 1990s, the government offered non-means-tested loan scheme to cover tuition fees and (in some cases) living costs for students not eligible for means-tested grants. Singapore provides non-need-based student grants. A Tuition Grant Scheme (TGS) was introduced by the Government in 1980 to subsidize the cost of tertiary education and is open to students enrolled in full-time diploma or undergraduate courses at fourteen institutions (Ministry of Education Singapore 2015). According to the report of Singapore Ministry of Education, for public higher education institutions in 2015, tuition fees for Singaporean students ranged from S$2100 (approximately £1100) to S$18,960 (approximately £9950). The average level was S$6620 (approximately £3475).

Studying at a national university in Taiwan costs around £1330 a year, and around £2450 is needed for private universities (Minister of Education Taiwan, 2013). Taiwan has also capped tuition fees at Taiwanese universities (Marcucci and Usher 2011), but the financial aid policy is more complex as it operates as a set of subsidies with different target groups, including student loans, subsidies for students with low incomes or unemployed parents and aboriginal students. In 2009, the grant was 5000 TWD

Table 4. Tertiary education 2010.

Cases	Higher education (the level of tuition fees/financial assistance)	Fuzzy scores
China	Moderate/strict selective	0.42
Hong Kong	Low/not selective	1
Japan	High/strict selective	0.32
Korea	High/strict selective financial aid and non-selective loan	0.65
Singapore	Low/not selective	0.98
Taiwan	Low/selective	0.72

Table 5. Education service fuzzy-set scores.

Cases	Spending in education service (S)	Generosity of education service (G)	Accessibility of education (A)	Education in ideal-type analysis (Minimum of S, G, and A)
China	0.40	0.82	0.42	0.40
Hong Kong	0.89	1	1	0.89
Japan	0	0.82	0.32	0
Korea	0.51	0.75	0.65	0.51
Singapore	1	0.78	0.98	0.78
Taiwan	1	0.82	0.72	0.72

(approximately £110) for a student in a public higher education institution and 8000 TWD (approximately £175) for a student in a private higher education institution. Since 2005, students from low-income families can also apply for free housing. Moreover, Taiwan also has some specially targeted subsidy programmes, such as grants for students with parents who work as civil servants, soldiers and faculty members, and for children of farmers and fishermen. As well as these grants, student loans are also available for students from middle- and low-income families, and were expanded in 2003 to cover high-income families with more than two children in higher education. After this reform, more than half of the families were eligible for the loan. Table 4 gives a brief overall summary of the tuition fees and financial assistance in the six cases. Table 5 provides the fuzzy set scores for the three sub-indicators, S, G and A, for the education set.

Findings and discussion

To combine sub-indicators to form education, health care services, family, old-age pensions, housing and protective labour market policy sets respectively, the intersection rule (also called the minimum principle) was used. In other words, the value of education set (E) in S*A*G is the minimum value of V^s, V^a and V^g. Table 6 shows the fuzzy-set score of the education service in the cases under consideration. Following a similar process,

Table 6. Fuzzy scores of six welfare dimensions.

Cases	Education service (E)	Health service (H)	Family policy (F)	Old-age income protection (I)	Public housing policy (P)	Passive labour market policy (L)
China	0.40	0.51	0.54	0.17	0.41	0.45
Hong Kong	0.89	0.06	0.47	0.61	1	0
Japan	0	1	0.41	0.64	0.36	0.13
Korea	0.51	0.68	0.57	0.74	0.55	0.46
Singapore	0.78	0.01	0.70	0.02	1	0
Taiwan	0.72	0.21	0.48	0.87	0.10	0.70

Table 7. Welfare models of the six cases.

Cases	Welfare models
China	Weak productive model (eHFipl 0.51)
Hong Kong	Weak protective balanced model (EhflP 0.53)
Japan	Residual balanced model (eHflpl 0.59)
Korea	Productive balanced model (EHFIPI 0.51)
Singapore	Weak productive balanced model (EhFiPl 0.7)
Taiwan	Weak protective balance welfare (EhflpL 0.52)

the other policy fields were transformed into fuzzy sets for each East Asian case study in this paper. Finally, the membership scores of the ideal types were also calculated based on the minimum principle. The highest membership score (>0.5) among the ideal types denotes each case's welfare model. Table 7 sums up the welfare models of the six cases in 2010.

The FSITA results show that there are clear and important differences between the welfare systems of the six cases in Greater China and East Asia. They are clustered into five distinctive welfare models and even for those that are classified in the same welfare model, such as Taiwan and Hong Kong, their ideal type membership is diverse. Most cases cluster into the 'balanced welfare model', which indicates that these cases have extended both their productive and their protective dimensions in recent years. Only China has maintained a productive welfare model according to the FsITA analysis that is largely in line with recent appraisals of Chinese welfare pragmatism (Mok 2016). While contrary to the PWC thesis, these findings are in accordance with scholars' that have argued East Asian welfare systems have generally become more redistributive after the Asian financial crisis in 1997. But how could we explain this apparent policy divergence? At least three possible reasons can be advanced as follows.

First, *historical legacy matters*: as two former British colonies Hong Kong and Singapore emphasize public housing as an instrument of economic growth. The Housing Authority of the colonial governments built numerous public rental and home-ownership estates and as a result, the public housing systems of Hong Kong and Singapore are outstanding in East Asia. Second, *economic strategy matters*: the export-oriented economic strategy of Korea and Taiwan shaped their social policies to focus more heavily on core industrial workers. In comparison, the economic strategy of Singapore, for instance, is very different. The goal of the People's Action Party (PAP) was to build Singapore as an international entrepôt that provides generous tax incentives and allows international capital to own their business operations completely (Chua 2005). Hence, the Central Provident Fund (CPF) was designed to only cover those employed. As the CPF is fully funded by contributions, the welfare system does not involve redistribution mechanism in Singapore, which is a significant competitive advantage for Singapore as an international platform for business. Third, *demographic change matters*: low fertility rates and an aging population have become a serious social issue in East Asia. In response to these challenges, a number of reforms have been launched. For instance, maternity leave benefits were expanded to cover more than two children in Singapore and the duration of the leave was extended to the ILO standard in 2008. Similarly, China has abolished its one-child policy in 2015. Japan has raised the official retirement age from 55 to 60 in 1998, and the government has decided to raise it further to 65 in 2025.

Although there is clear divergence across Greater China and East Asia, it is undeniable that some similarities between these welfare systems continue to exist. First, productivism is still an important feature in East Asia as all observed cases possess relatively high degrees of membership in at least one productive welfare dimension. Some productive features continue to stand out as particularly significant. Four of the six states are 'in' the set of education and the relatively high public spending on education is particularly worth noting. Similarly, public expenditure on health care and the coverage of public health care system is also comparatively high. Second, the protective features of the welfare systems are also substantial in some cases and particularly the welfare systems of Hong Kong and Taiwan were more protective than productive. The majority of cases were clustered into the balanced welfare model indicating memberships to both productive and protective dimensions, but it is worth mentioning that most cases began to emphasize social protection in one way or another. Pension systems in China, Hong Kong, Korea, and Taiwan have seen major reforms since the 2000s. Korea and Taiwan have even introduced universal non-contributory based pension programmes. However, most other welfare programmes remain insurance based and/or are funded by individual contributions, and state intervention is therefore limited. In particular, private health expenditures in the region remain high and the use of provident funds in Singapore and Hong Kong suggests that the role of fully funded welfare programmes remains important. Third, and finally, culture remains an important factor to help understand the welfare ideology in the region. One significant difference between the East and the West is the argument that families play a major role in providing social support in traditional Chinese cultural society compared with the religious philanthropy of the West. As the family continues to act as an important provider of welfare, the role of social policy continues to be limited and primarily used for preserving social stability (Chau and Yu 2005).

Conclusion

The paper set out to re-examine two major research questions that have dominated East Asian social policy analysis: first, does East Asia have a homogenous welfare model; and second, if so, can this model still sensibly be regarded as productivist? Based on the analysis carried out in this paper, the short and simple answer to both questions is 'no'.

Although several researchers have argued for a homogenous productivist East Asian welfare model, the FsITA findings of this paper provide limited support for this thesis. Instead, while East Asian welfare systems share some common characteristics, the intra-diversity between them is significant. Six different ideal types of welfare system were found to belong to five welfare models combining productive and protective intent to various degrees. The results also show that the level of welfare development in the region is very different. Among the six observed cases, Korea had the overall most comprehensive welfare policies, while Japan's welfare state retrogressed relatively speaking. In short, the East Asian welfare systems are increasingly divergent: not only in terms of their emphasis on particular welfare services, but also in terms of their respective levels of development.

Although the findings show that productivism is an important feature in East Asia – in fact, it is striking that all the six cases possess relatively high degrees of membership of at least one productive welfare dimension – it should be noted that the protective features of the welfare systems are also substantial in some cases. In particular, the welfare systems of Hong Kong and Taiwan were more protective than productive. Among the six cases, only China did not show any protective characteristics, and the majority of cases were clustered into the balanced welfare model indicating memberships to both productive and protective dimensions. The findings of this paper therefore demonstrate that it is inaccurate to conclude that East Asian welfare systems are merely productive.

While the empirical findings of this paper are based on a new theoretical and analytical framework, it was argued that by employing FsITA analysis the data availability issues in East Asian welfare research can be overcome. Indeed, this paper demonstrates that FsITA is particularly suitable for comparative welfare research in East Asian context. An important advantage is that it can overcome the data availability issues in East Asian welfare research by allowing the simultaneous assessment of quantitative data and qualitative cases. It is in this sense, that the paper provides a starting point for further systematic comparative discussions on welfare developments in East Asia. Comparative East Asian social policy analysis has much to gain from incorporating FsITA and other set-theoretic techniques into its methodological toolkit more frequently.

Notes

1. Many studies have shown that child care provision also has positive impact on female participation in developed countries. However, the availability of data issue is significant in measuring child care provision, especially in the East Asian context. Hence, maternity leave is used solely in this paper.
2. All fuzzy scores of quantitative data were generated by R (R Core Team 2014) and using the QCA (Dusa and Alrik 2014) and SetMethods packages, respectively (Quaranta 2013b).
3. In 2011, a plan for twelve years of compulsory curriculum was developed in Taiwan. In 2012, the project was audited and it was finally implemented in 2014 (Ministry of Education Taiwan 2013).

Acknowledgements

A previous version of this article was presented at the EASP annual conference in Singapore 2015. Thanks to all participants in the conference for useful comments. Also, as this paper was part of my PhD project, I would like to express my special gratitude to my supervisor Prof. Stefan Kühner for his very helpful suggestions and comments.

Disclosure statement

No potential conflict of interest was reported by the author.

References

ADB, 2012. *Key Indicators for Asia and the Pacific 2012*. Philippines: Asian Development Bank.

Addati, L., Cassirer, N., and Gilchrist, K., 2014. *Maternity and paternity at work: law and practice across the world*. Geneva: International Labour Office.

Altbach, P., 2006. *Financing higher education*. Rotterdam, the Netherlands: Sense.

Aspalter, C., 2005. The welfare state in East Asia: an ideal-typical welfare regime. *Journal of Societal & Social Policy*, 4/1, 1–20.

Aspalter, C., 2006. The East Asian welfare model. *International Journal of Social Welfare*, 15 (4), 290–301. doi:10.1111/ijsw.2006.15.issue-4

Aspalter, C., 2011. The development of ideal-typical welfare regime theory. *International Social Work*, 54 (6), 735–750. doi:10.1177/0020872810393765

Baker, M. and Milligan, K., 2008. How does job-protected maternity leave affect mothers' employment? *Journal of Labor Economics*, 26 (4), 655–691. doi:10.1086/591955

Brhane, M., Mason, D., and Payne, G., 2014. *Access to affordable and low-income housing in East Asia and the Pacific*. Washington, DC: Word Bank Group.

Carneiro, P., Loken, K., and Salvanes, K. 2011. A flying start? Maternity leave benefits and long run outcomes of children. IZA Discussion Paper No. 5793

Cerise, S., et al., 2013. *How do maternity leave and discriminatory social norms relate to women's employment in developing countries?* Paris: OECD Development Centre.

Chau, R.C.M. and Yu, W.K., 2005. Is welfare unAsian? In: A. Walker and C.K. Wong, eds. *East Asian welfare regimes in transition*. Bristol: The Policy Press.

Chua, B.H., 2005. Welfare developmentalism in Singapore and Malaysia. In: H.J. Kwon, ed. *Transforming the developmental welfare state in East Asia*. London: Palgrave Macmillan UK, 98–117.

Dusa, A. and Alrik, T. 2014. QCA: a package for qualitative comparative analysis. R package version 1.1-3.

Esping-Andersen, G., 1990. *The three worlds of welfare capitalism*. Cambridge: Polity Press.

Esping-Andersen, G., 1997. Hybrid or unique? The Japanese welfare state between Europe and America. *Journal of European Social Policy*, 7 (3), 179. doi:10.1177/095892879700700301

Feng, J.Y. and Han, W.-J., 2010. Maternity leave in Taiwan. *Family Relations*, 59 (3), 297–312. doi:10.1111/fare.2010.59.issue-3

Fu, T.H. and Hughes, R., 2009. Introduction: challenges to population ageing in East Asia. In: T.H. Fu and R. Hughes, eds. *Ageing in East Asia: challenges and policies for the twenty-first century*. Abingdon: Routledge, 1–14.

Goodman, R. and Peng, I., 1996. The East Asian welfare states: peripatetic learning, adaptive change, and nation-building. In: G. Esping-Andersen, ed. *Welfare states in transition: national adaptations in global economies*. London: Sage, 192–224.

Goodman, R., White, G., and Kwon, H., 1997. East Asian social policy: a model to emulate? In: M. May, E. Brunsdon and G. Esping-Andersen, eds. *Social Policy Review 9*. Canterbury: Social Policy Association, 359–380.

Goodman, R., White, G., and Kwon, H., 1998. *The East Asian welfare model: welfare orientalism and the state*. London: Routledge.

Gough, I., 2001. Globalization and regional welfare regimes. *Global Social Policy*, 1 (2), 163. doi:10.1177/146801810100100202

Gough, I., 2004. East Asia: the limits of productivist regimes. In: I. Gough and G. Wood, eds. *Insecurity and welfare regimes in Asia, Africa and Latin America: social policy development contexts*. Cambridge: Cambridge University Press, 169–201.

Hill, M.J., 1996. *Social policy: a comparative analysis*. New York: Prentice-Hall/Harvester Wheatsheaf.

Hoekstra, J., 2003. Housing and the welfare state in the Netherlands: an application of Esping-Andersen's typology. *Housing, Theory and Society*, 20 (2), 58–71. doi:10.1080/14036090310000634

Holliday, I., 2000. Productivist welfare capitalism: social policy in East Asia. *Political Studies*, 48 (4), 706–723. doi:10.1111/1467-9248.00279

Holliday, I., 2005. East Asian social policy in the wake of the financial crisis: farewell to productivism? *Policy & Politics*, 33 (1), 145–162. doi:10.1332/0305573052708465

Holliday, I. and Wilding, P., 2003. *Welfare capitalism in East Asia: social policy in the tiger economies*. Basingstoke: Palgrave Macmillan.

Hudson, J. and Kühner, S., 2009. Towards productive welfare? A comparative analysis of 23 OECD countries. *Journal of European Social Policy*, 19 (1), 34–46. doi:10.1177/0958928708098522

Hudson, J. and Kühner, S., 2010. Beyond the dependent variable problem: the methodological challenges of capturing productive and protective dimensions of social policy. *Social Policy and Society*, 9 (2), 167–179. doi:10.1017/S1474746409990327

Hudson, J., and Kühner, S., 2012. Analyzing the productive and protective dimensions of welfare: looking beyond the oecd. *Social Policy & Administration*, 46 (1), 35-60. doi: 10.1111/j.1467-9515.2011.00813.x

ILO, 2016. *Health Services Sector* [online]. Available from: http://www.ilo.org/global/industries-and-sectors/health-services/lang-en/index.htm [Accessed 30 March 2016].

JASSO, 2014. *JASSO Supports Motivated and Capable Students* [online]. [Last updated 5 October 2014]. Available from: http://www.jasso.go.jp/about_jasso/documents/e2014_05_09.pdf [Accessed 19 May 2015].

Jaumotte, F. 2003. Female labour force participation: past trends and main determinants in OECD countries. OECD Economics Deparment Working Papers. Paris: OECD.

Kemeny, J., 2001. Comparative housing and welfare: theorising the relationship. *Journal of Housing and the Built Environment*, 16 (1), 53–70. doi:10.1023/A:1011526416064

Kim, Y.-M., 2008. Beyond East Asian welfare productivism in South Korea. *Policy & Politics*, 36 (1), 109–125. doi:10.1332/030557308783431652

Ku, Y., 1997. *Welfare capitalism in Taiwan: state, economy and social policy*. Basingstoke: Palgrave Macmillan.

Kuhnle, S., 2004. Productive welfare in Korea: moving towards a European welfare state type? In: R. Mishra, et al., eds. *Modernizing the Korean welfare state: towards the productive welfare model*. New Brunswick, NJ: Transaction, 47–64.

Kvist, J., 1999. Welfare reform in the Nordic countries in the 1990s: using fuzzy-set theory to assess conformity to ideal types. *Journal of European Social Policy*, 9 (3), 231–252. doi:10.1177/095892879900900303

Kvist, J., 2007. Fuzzy set ideal type analysis. *Journal of Business Research*, 60 (5), 474–481. doi:10.1016/j.jbusres.2007.01.005

Kwon, H., 2005. Transforming the developmental welfare state in East Asia. *Development and Change*, 36 (3), 477–497. doi:10.1111/dech.2005.36.issue-3

Lee, J., 2010. Deciphering productivism and developmentalism in East Asian social welfare. In: J. Lee and K.W. Chan, eds. *The crisis of welfare in East Asia*. Plymouth: Lexington Books, 1–26.

Lee, Y.-J. and Ku, Y., 2007. East Asian welfare regimes: testing the hypothesis of the developmental welfare state. *Social Policy & Administration*, 41 (2), 197–212. doi:10.1111/spol.2007.41.issue-2

Marcucci, P. and Usher, A., 2011. *Tuition fees and student financial assistance: 2010 global year in review*. Toronto: Higher Education Strategy Associates.

Ministry of Education Singapore, 2015. *TG online* [online]. Singapore: Ministry of Education. Available from: https://tgonline.moe.gov.sg/tgis/normal/index.action [Accessed 12 May 2016].

Ministry of Education Taiwan, 2013. *Higher education in Taiwan 2012-2013*. Taiwan: Chiang Wei-Ning (Minister of Education).

Mishra, R., 1995. Social security in South Korea and Singapore: explaining the differences. *Social Policy & Administration*, 29 (3), 228–240. doi:10.1111/j.1467-9515.1995.tb00466.x

Misra, J., Budig, M., and Boeckmann, I., 2011. Work-family policies and the effects of children on women's employment hours and wages. *Community, Work & Family*, 14 (2), 139–157. doi:10.1080/13668803.2011.571396

Mok, K.H. 2016. Social policy expansion and welfare regime(s) in transition: productivist construction of selective welfare capitalism in China. Paper under review by *Social Policy and Administration*.

Newby, H., et al., 2009. *OECD reviews of tertiary education: Japan*. Paris: OECD.

OECD, 2012. *Education at a Glance 2012*. Paris: OECD.

Packard, T.G. and Nguyen, T.V. 2014. *East Asia Pacific at work: employment, enterprise, and well-being*. World Bank East Asia and Pacific Regional Report. Washington, DC: The World Bank.

Quaranta, M. 2013a. Concept structures and fuzzy set theory: a proposal for concept formation and operationalization. *Comparative Sociology*, 2 (6), 785-820, 10.1163/15691330-12341283

Quaranta, M., 2013b. Setmethods: a package companion to "set-theoretic methods for the social sciences". *R Package Version*, 1.0.

R Core Team, 2014. *R: a language and environment for statistical computing*. Vienna, Austria.

Ragin, C.C., 2000. *Fuzzy-set social science*. London: University of Chicago Press.

Ramesh, M., 2004. *Social policy in East and Southeast Asia: education, health, housing, and income maintenance*. London: Routledge.

Rudra, N., 2007. Welfare states in developing countries: unique or universal? *The Journal of Politics*, 69 (2), 378–396. doi:10.1111/j.1468-2508.2007.00538.x

Takahashi, M., 1997. *The emergence of welfare society in Japan*. Aldershot: Avebury.

Tang, K.L., 1998. *Colonial state and social policy: social welfare development in Hong Kong 1842-1997*. Oxford: University Press of America.

The Korea Times, 2009. Study now, pay later: new lending system marks change in right direction. *The Korea Times* [online]. Available from: http://www.koreatimes.co.kr/www/news/opinon/2013/03/202_49420.html [Accessed 2 April 2015].

Thévenon, O. and Solaz, A., 2013. *Parental leave and labour market outcomes: lessons from 40 years of policies in OECD countries*. Paris: Institut national d'etudes demographiques.

University Grants Committee, 2010. *Aspirations for the higher education system in Hong Kong: report of the University Grants Committee*. Hong Kong: University Grants Committee.

Walker, A. and Wong, C.K., 2005. *East Asian welfare regimes in transition: from Confucianism and globalisation*. Bristol: Policy Press.

Wang, Y., 2012. *China social security system development report (2012)*. Beijing: Social Science Academic Press..

Wilding, P., 2008. Is the East Asian welfare model still productive? *Journal of Asian Public Policy*, 1 (1), 18–31. doi:10.1080/17520840701835815

Wilensky, H.L., 1975. *The welfare state and equality: structural and ideological roots of public expenditures*. London: University of California Press.

Index

Note: **Boldface** page numbers refer to tables & italic page numbers refer to figures. Page numbers followed by "n" refer to endnotes.

active labour market policies 12, 18
ADB (2013) 42
Adjusted Family Income (AFI) 113
anti-money laundering policies 18, 19
anti-poverty programme 47, 51
Apni Beti Apna Dhan 48
Argentinian political culture 17
Asian social policy: analysis 1; development processes 2
Awami League 35

'backward' gender welfare regime 70
'bailout' agreements 19
balanced welfare model 108, **109**
Balika Samridhi Yojana scheme 48
Bangladesh 32, 33; co-financed schemes 28; employment programme in 33
Benazir Income Support Programme (BISP) 32, 34
Bismarckian old-age insurance system 68
BISP *see* Benazir Income Support Programme
Boli, Thomas 2
Bretton Woods System 58

Cairo Conference on Population and Development 17, 18
cash transfer programmes, India 48
Central Benefit Agency 65
Central Provident Fund (CPF) 115
central reform policy, in Germany 69
central state regulatory agency 64
"Chameleon" Korean Welfare Regime 100
childcare, impact on issues of 67–9
child-oriented pension policy 60
China 94–5, 110; German pension reforms for 69–70; social decentralization in 76–8; social security systems 74
Chinese cultural society 116
Chinese pension systems 58, 69

Chinese politics 75
Chinese social policy 76
Chinese social security reforms 85
Chinese style central–local relationship 5
coercion 19, 28
coercive conditionality 19
coercive transfers 11
cognitive harmonization 18
Communist party 80, 85
community-care voucher program 98
competitive solidarity 76, 79–80, 85–6
Comprehensive Peace Agreement (CPA) 32
Confucian, East Asian welfare regime 93–4
Confucianism 95, 100
Confucian welfare regime 94
Confucian welfare states 90
Congress-led coalition 31
Congress party 31
Congress/United Progressive Alliance 41
consensual transfers 11
contribution-free social schemes 26
CPA *see* Comprehensive Peace Agreement
CPF *see* Central Provident Fund

deepening reforms 82, 83, 86
direct cash transfer scheme 34
domestic violence 46
double bargaining process 17
drastic demographic transition 60

Early Childhood Education Services 95
East Asian productivist welfare capitalism 104, 105
East Asian tiger economies 40
East Asian welfare model **109**; Asian financial crisis 104; conceptualizing 105–8; East Asian productivist welfare capitalism 104; re-examining using fuzzy sets, 108–14
East Asian welfare regime 93; Confucian 93–4; productivist 91–3; proliferation and status of care policies in 94–9; welfare modelling business 90
East Asia, social policy in 91

INDEX

economic globalization 92
education, India's investment in 42
education service fuzzy-set scores **114**
EES *see* European Employment Strategy
EGPP *see* employment programme
empirical cluster analyses 43
Employment Guarantee Programme 33
employment programme (EGPP) 34, 35; in Bangladesh 33
EU *see* European Union
European Central Bank 19
European Council 19
European Economic Community 79
European Employment Strategy (EES) 17
European single-market project 79
European Social Model 19
European style welfare states 92
European Union (EU): Open Method of Coordination 17; social policy 79; wide policy development 17
experimentation-based policy cycle 75

family, impact on issues of 67–9
family-oriented pension policy 60
family policies 106
FATF *see* Financial Action Task Force
Federal Financial Supervisory Authority (FFSA) 64
Federal Republic of Germany 57
FFSA *see* Federal Financial Supervisory Authority
Financial Action Task Force (FATF) 18, 19
Financial Intelligence Units 19
Food for Work 33
Fourth World Conference on Women 18
Freedom of Information Law 13
free education 110
FSITA *see* fuzzy-set ideal-type analysis
funded pension 58–9; in German **66**
fuzzy-set ideal-type analysis (FSITA) 42, 105, 108

Gateway Review Process 15
gender-based model 68
gender, impact on issues of 67–9
gender-neutral pension policy, in Germany 70
German pension reforms 57–9, 61; change in policy instruments and policy ideas 60–3; for China 69–70; demographic transition and its impact on discourses of 60; as family, childcare and gender policy 59–60; funded pension 58–9; German-style funded pension 63–70
German pension system 57, 61, 63, 66, 69; gender-neutral policy 70; partial privatization of 65; supervisory regime 65
German social insurance system 62
German statutory pension insurance scheme 60, 69

German-style of funded pension 63–70
German welfare state 58, 70n1
global economic governance 16
global institutions policy 18
globalization 13
global policy chains 16
Global Strategy for Women's and Children's Health 47
global welfare regime clusters **56**
Green Party 63

Hartz IV reform 70n1
health care 106
Hong Kong 98
household registration system 82
hukou system 82
human capital investment 41

ICDS *see* Integrated Child Development Programme
IDA *see* International Development Assistance
ILO *see* International Labour Organisation
IMF *see* International Monetary Fund
inclusive model 92
INC *see* Indian National Congress
Income Transfer Scheme for Girls with Insurance Cover 48
Independent Administrative Institution Japan Student Services Organisation (JASSO) 113
India: cash transfer programmes 48; democracy 52; economic development 40; investment in education 42; transformative social protection in 48–51
Indian constitution 51
Indian National Congress (INC) 31
Indian social policy innovations 51
Indian welfare regime 41, 43–6; in literature 42–3; productive-protective policies of 47; revisited 43–6
India's emerging social policy paradigm 40–1, 46–8; Indian welfare regime in literature 42–3; Indian welfare regime revisited 43–6; transformative social protection in India 48–51
Indira Gandhi National Old Age Pension Scheme (NOAPS) 46
informal policy networks 13
informal security regimes 43
Integrated Child Development Programme (ICDS) 46
inter-generational contract 60
International Development Assistance (IDA) 33
International Labour Organisation (ILO) 16, 58; classification 45
international law 18
International Monetary Fund (IMF) 11
International World Summit for Children 18
ITSGIC 50

INDEX

Janani Suraksha Yojana 47
Jan Dhan Yojana programme 52
Japan 95–6

Kasturba Gandhi Balika Vidyalay 48
Korea 96–7
Korean welfare state 92, 104, 105
Kühner 4

labour-intensive industries 81
labour market informality 47
labour market programmes 44
lazy allowance 33
liberal regime 99, 100
Long Term Care Insurance (LTCI) 91, 95, 96
Lui 4–5

Maharashtra Employment Guarantee Scheme (MEGS) 36n2
Mahatma Gandhi Rural Employment Guarantee Act (MGNREGA) 29, 33, 35, 47, 50, 51
'masculine' pension system 69
MDGs *see* Millennium Development Goals
MEGS *see* Maharashtra Employment Guarantee Scheme
Meyer, John 2
MGNREGA *see* Mahatma Gandhi Rural Employment Guarantee Act
Millennium Development Goals (MDGs) 18
Minimum Living Standard Scheme 81
mobile capital, competition for 28
modern pension system 59
Modi, Narendra 51–2
Mukhyamantri Balika Cycle Yojana 48

Nakray 4
national employment guarantee scheme 32
national employment program, differences and similarities 29–31
National Food Security Act (NFSA) 46
National Health Insurance Programme 47
National Programme for Education of Girls at Elementary-Level 48
National Rural Health Mission (NHM) 47
National Sample Survey (NSS) 46
National Social Protection Strategy 32
neoliberal grand reform 58
Nepal 32–4
'New Right' Conservative government 3
new social cash-transfer programmes/minimum-income schemes 27
new social schemes in South Asia 26
NFSA *see* National Food Security Act
NHM *see* National Rural Health Mission
non-adoption employment programmes 27
non-contributory basic pension 71n7
non-state actors 12
NSS *see* National Sample Survey

'Oiconomic welfare states' 90
old-age income protection 106
old-age pension insurance 68
one-child policy 70
Organisation for Economic Co-operation and Development (OECD) countries 12, 18, 107
Ozkan's exploration 19

Pakistan 32, 34
Pakistan People's Party (PPP) 32
passive labour market policy 107
pay-as-you-go (PAYG) system 57, 58, 60
'pension market' 59
pension privatization 59
pension reforms: in China 71n7; in Germany *see* German pension reforms; policies 68
pension system in modern society 59
People's Action Party (PAP) 115
People's Republic of China (PRC) 93
PFI models *see* private finance initiative models
pilot scheme 34
PISA test 45
Planning Commission 42
PMI *see* power as mutual influence
policies and actors 11–14
policy convergence 2
policy diffusion, channels for 28–9
policy imposition 19
policy-making activity 10
policy transfer 8–11, 22; in Asia 1–6; and power 14–20
power as coercion 19–20
power as mutual influence (PMI) 14–16
power as weighted bargaining (PWB) 14, 16–19
PPP *see* Pakistan People's Party
PRC *see* People's Republic of China
prerequisites explanations 2
private finance initiative (PFI) models 20
private healthcare firms 20
'private pension sector' in Germany 64
private–public partnership (PPP) 20
productive–protective policies of Indian welfare regime 47
productive welfare models 107, **109**
productivism 107, 116
productivist model 92
"productivist reconstruction of solidarity" 79
productivist social policy 105–6
protective approach 48
protective welfare models 107, **109**
proto-natalist 17
"Provisionary Arrangement of Residence Document" 82
'public pension' 59
public–private sector collaborations 20
public sector infrastructure projects 20
public welfare state activity 42
PWB *see* power as weighted bargaining

123

INDEX

Rashtriya Madhyamik Shiksha Yojana 48
RCIW Programme *see* Rural Community Infrastructure Works Programme
redistributive model 92
'regional leadership role' 41
regional protectionism 82–3
'restricted policy transfer' 15
Retirement Assets Act 65
Riester pension 63, 66; contracts 65; investment products 64; operation of 65; payments 64; reform 57, 63–7, 70n1; scheme *64*, 68
Riester plan 58
rights-based social protection schemes 27, 28, 33
'rights-holders' citizens 27
robust model 10
RSBY 50, 51
Rural Community Infrastructure Works (RCIW) Programme 34
Rural Maintenance Programmes 33

self-reinforcing process 20
set-theoretic theory 107
Shi 5
Singapore 98–9; economic strategy of 115
social decentralization 85–6; central coordination and local implementation in social security 83–5; in China 76–8; China's social security systems 74; and competitive solidarity 79–80; regional competition and emulation 80–2; regional protectionism 82–3; urban–rural harmonization 74
Social Democratic Party (SPD) 63
"social-democratic" welfare regime 105
social insurance model 58
social market economy 67
social policy 78; development in China 84; diffusion in South Asia *see* South Asia, social policy diffusion in; in East Asia 91; innovations 41, 46, 48, 49; investments 92; learning 80; programmes 32; reforms of Germany 70
social protection: policies 42; programmes 51; schemes 27
social security: policies 2; programmes 79, 81, 82; reform 83
social solidarity in China 86
social transfer schemes 25
socio-economic 'prerequisites' 4
"soft centralization" 75
South Asia, social policy diffusion in: channels for policy diffusion 28–9; national employment programmes, differences and similarities between 29–31; neighbouring countries 31–4; policy diffusion as potential explanation of programme spread 27–8; social transfer schemes 25; widening income inequality and new social protection paradigm 26–7
SPD *see* Social Democratic Party
Special Administrative Region (SAR) of China 105
state-level programmes 48
statutory pension insurance 66; scheme 63
stratified social welfare system 67
"supply-side reforms" 86

Taiwan 97–8
Targeted Public Distribution System (TPDS) 46
"tax-assignment" reform 78
tax-financed health insurance schemes 27
Tertiary Student Finance Scheme (TSFS) 113
TFR *see* total fertility rate
TGS *see* Tuition Grant Scheme
TIMMS test 45
total fertility rate (TFR) 60
Township Insurance Scheme 81
TPDS *see* Targeted Public Distribution System
traditional employment programmes 28
traditional social insurance 33; programmes 25
traditional welfare states 105
transformative social protection in India 48–51
TSFS *see* Tertiary Student Finance Scheme
Tuition Grant Scheme (TGS) 113
Turkey's Unemployment Insurance (UI) scheme 19
Turkish advocacy coalitions 20
Turkish civil service 20
Turkish economic bureaucracy 20

underdeveloped welfare **109**
Unemployment Insurance (UI) scheme, Turkey 19
United Nations Resolution on Sustainable Development 41
universal pension scheme 31
'universal programme' 50
urban–rural harmonization 74, 81

'weak productive–protective' 43
welfare modelling business 42, 106
welfare models 108, *108*
welfare state: arrangements 59; regimes 43, 91
welfare system, in Korea 104
welfare tourism 83
wider-ranging approach 8
World Bank (WB) 11, 33, 42, 45, 58, 63, 66, 71n7; multi-pillar insurance models **66**; publication 58

Yang 5

zero tolerance criminal justice policies 15